24

QUESTIONS
IN GROUP
LEADERSHIP

24
QUESTIONS IN GROUP LEADERSHIP

SECOND EDITION

ERNEST D. NATHAN
Management Consultant

CARTOONS BY JOHNNY SAJEM

ADDISON–WESLEY PUBLISHING COMPANY
Reading, Massachusetts · Menlo Park, California
London · Amsterdam · Don Mills, Ontario · Sydney

The first edition of this work was entitled
TWENTY QUESTIONS ON CONFERENCE LEADERSHIP

Library of Congress Cataloging in Publication Data

Nathan, Ernest D
    24 questions in group leadership.

    Published in 1969 under title: Twenty questions
on conference leadership.
    Bibliography: p.
    1. Meetings. I. Title.
AS6.N3 1979   658.4'56   78-73371
    ISBN 0-201-05263-6

ISBN 0-201-5263-6
ABCDEFGHIJ-AL-79

ACKNOWLEDGMENTS
AND THANKS

My thanks to many group members and leaders who have contributed, often unknowingly, to the ideas expressed in this book—and in the formulation of the questions and the development of the answers.

Special thanks go to Dr. Ralph G. Nichols, Professor Emeritus, University of Minnesota, who encouraged me to write about the use of questions in group leadership; to Dr. Raymond S. Ross, Professor of Speech, Wayne State University, who has given me guidance as teacher and friend; and to Dr. James P. Dee, formerly Professor of Industrial Communication, Bowling Green State University and now Chief, Field Operations Unit, Training Section, United Nations Industrial Development Organization.

Also, my appreciation to Julian W. Moody, management counsellor; George W. Martin, Manpower Development Specialist, Blue Cross/Blue Shield of Michigan; and Dale J. Madden, communications specialist, for their contributions along the way. All are gifted group leaders and practitioners of learning through discussion.

My warm thanks also go to Gen Florez and other members of the Florez Organization who have stimulated my interest in the dynamics of group leadership.

Detroit, Michigan   E. D. N.
March 1979

INTRODUCTION

This is a working handbook for supervisors, staff members, and managers at all levels who often find themselves in the role of group meeting leader, and who are looking for ways to improve their leadership skills. For you, this book is designed to help get the results you want from the conferences, seminars, or workshops you hold and, more likely than not, the results your management expects.

This book is built around a number of questions frequently asked about group meeting leadership. The answers are by no means absolute, but they have proved helpful to others who are concerned about perfecting their leadership skills.

WHAT IS GROUP MEETING LEADERSHIP?

Before setting out to answer the questions, let's answer the underlying question, "What *is* group meeting leadership?" As a group leader, it may be your responsibility to plan, organize, and conduct many types of group meetings. It's possible that the meeting may be a simple gathering to exchange the latest "scoop" at the water cooler. Or it may be a planned weekend affair at a ski lodge.

Whether long or short, all group meetings we know about in a business or professional context have at least one thing in common: they are discussions in which groups of people with common interests interchange ideas to reach given objectives, usually under leadership.

KINDS OF GROUP MEETINGS

Many different terms are used to describe group meetings. Let's look at some of them:

- **CONFERENCE**

    Conference is a very broad term that means different things to different people. To *Webster* it means, "Formal consultation or discussion, an interchange of views, a meeting." *American Heritage Dictionary* says, "A meeting for consultation or discussion."

    To me a conference, as the word implies, is a session in which people confer—an exchange of ideas for mutual benefit under leadership. It's a bit more formal than just a plain "meeting." A conference is usually announced in advance for a specific time and place and has a stated purpose or subject.

    But as David Berlo puts it, "Meanings are not found in words at all, they are found only in people."* So probably the most important definition of all is the definition *you* give it.

- **SEMINAR**

    Webster: A group of students (usually graduate students) engaged, under a professor, in original research.

---

*David K. Berlo, 1960. *The Process of Communication*. New York: Holt, Rinehart and Winston, p. 174.

American Heritage: (1) a small group of advanced students in a college or graduate school engaged in original research under the guidance of a professor who meets regularly with them for reports and discussions. (2) A meeting for exchange of ideas in some area: conference.

To me a seminar is more formal than a conference and is generally built around a presentation or talk by an authority on the subject followed by discussion.

- **WORKSHOP**

   Webster: A shop where any manufacture or handiwork is carried on.

   American Heritage: (2) A group of people who meet regularly for a seminar in some specialized field.

To me a workshop is a small group meeting where the emphasis is on identifying or solving problems and, through exercises, cases, and instruments of various kinds, working out practical answers.

What do "conference," "seminar," and "workshop," mean to you? The decision is up to you. In this book, for simplicity's sake, we'll call all these kinds of meetings *conferences.*

KINDS OF CONFERENCES

We've all attended different kinds of conferences although probably no one bothered to label them other than just plain "conference." Regardless of the label, group meetings like these are generally held for one of the following reasons:

- *To identify a problem or need:* The leader states the purpose of the meeting. Then through questioning, directs the group members to a meaningful conclusion.
- *To solve a problem:* The leader presents the problem and all members of the group, including the leader, put their heads together to work out a solution.

- *To give information:* The leader states the subject of the meeting and presents the necessary information to the group.

- *To get information:* The leader presents the subject and then calls on group members to contribute their ideas.

- *To brainstorm:* The group is asked to think about a given subject or problem for a few minutes, and then come up with as many ideas as it can—the wilder the better. A recorder notes all ideas produced. After the session is over the ideas are sorted out and evaluated.

- *To guide to a conclusion:* The leader has a program, a product, a procedure, or a point of view to "sell" to the group. This kind of session might well be called a "group sale." In this book we'll call it a "guided conference."

Think back over the meetings you have held or attended during the past year. Whether they were called "conferences," "seminars," or "workshops," the chances are most of them were "guided" to some degree. As we all know, this is because business meetings are held to sell ideas, and group leaders are judged by their batting averages in achieving their objectives.

GETTING THE RIGHT THINGS DONE

In these days when "knowledge workers" are replacing "manual workers" at appalling speed, group leadership—the ability to make a group sale whether in a conference, a seminar, a workshop, or a meeting of any kind—has become a required management skill. The effective executive, Peter Drucker writes, is one "who is expected to get the right things done."* To get the right things done, the group leader must be able to get the results expected through others. If this book helps you "get the right things done" through more effective guided conferences, it will have achieved its purpose.

---

*Peter Drucker, 1966. *The Effective Executive*. New York: Harper & Row, p. 1.

CONTENTS

QUESTION 1

WHAT IS A "GUIDED CONFERENCE" AND HOW DOES IT DIFFER FROM OTHER KINDS OF CONFERENCES?

To some extent all true conferences are "guided" conferences. They have a leader to keep things on the track and a purpose to achieve. Some conferences are held to explore an idea, solve a problem, or give or receive information. Yet you couldn't consider these to be guided conferences in the sense that the leader is trying to make a group sale.

Let's say, for example, that you are planning a conference to tackle a company problem that urgently needs a solution. You will want to provide enough information and guidance so that the group will concentrate its attention on the problem and not go off in unrelated directions. You make sure that the discussion stays on course, yet you allow enough leeway so that everyone is encouraged to participate.

To take another example, let's assume your conference purpose is to tell your group about a new service your company plans to offer and to get their reaction to it. You will make sure that everyone understands the new service, and you will encourage the group to say what they think of the plan. In this instance, you don't want to *influence* the thinking of the group; you just want to find out what it *is*.

In both cases, you provide some guidance, yet neither conference is a *guided conference* in the sense considered in this book.

If, on the other hand, your conference purpose is not only to *announce* the new service but also to *win the support* of the group for it, then, according to our concept, you are conducting a guided conference.

DEFINITION OF A GUIDED CONFERENCE

Let's define the guided conference as a group discussion in which the leader carries the responsibility for winning group acceptance for a predetermined (and often preannounced) objective. The leader imparts information as a basis for the meeting, then encourages discussion by the group, which he or she guides to a proper conclusion.

Now let's consider each of the main parts of this definition in terms of your activities and responsibilities as guided-conference leader.

A Group Discussion

Many a guided conference has fallen flat because this phrase was not understood. The word "group" is used in a homogeneous sense in that the members must have a community of interest in the subject of the discussion. Otherwise the people assembled are simply a hodgepodge, a heterogeneous gathering rather than a group. The results from this kind of miscellaneous audience will be far from encouraging.

The word "discussion" is also a key to the nature of the conference. If you plan simply to make a speech or a formal presentation and then open the meeting to questions to be answered by you, the expert, you are not within the range of the definition. Without the participation of the conferees and free exchange of ideas between them and the leader, the meeting is not a guided conference.

The Leader Carries the Responsibility

When you lead a guided conference, you are much more than just a "traffic cop" who sees that the discussion stays on the subject but who, in no way, enters the proceedings. Such a role is quite justified in some forms of brainstorming, problem solving, or information gathering. But in the guided conference, you, as leader, carry the responsibility for making sure that orderly progress is made toward your objective. You must, of course, be able to perform this function without dominating the conference. Obviously this takes advance planning, plenty of patience, and skillful use of all available conference tools. As in any other form of making a sale, you stimulate the interest of the group, provide needed information, and encourage participation. You also see that the conference stays on course. Here's an example.

- A conference is being planned in a large bank as this chapter is being written. It's purpose is to develop and gain acceptance for an organized plan for making sales calls on the bank's customers.

- Certain information must be gathered before the call can be made. Using the "buzz group" technique, with four or five to a group, the leader assigns each group the task of preparing a list of all the needed information and of the sources of that information.

- Each group reports its findings. These are listed on a chart pad and eventually arranged in logical order.

- The leader has taken the precaution of including in the written conference plan all the major types of information and their sources. Then the leader makes a quick check to make sure all the essential points are covered. If one has been omitted, a well-placed question will draw it from the group and it will become part of the conferees' thinking.

Wins Group Acceptance

The word "wins" is the key. As leader, you have the responsibility of *winning* group acceptance, not driving or coercing or tricking the group into accepting the idea. To do this you must be willing to listen to many different points of view, ask guiding questions, and not attempt to restrict or dictate the ideas of the conferees. As in the case of any other sale, the urge to buy comes from within.

Of a Predetermined Objective

If you are to accomplish the purpose of the conference, you should be clear on what the objective is *before* the conference begins. The best way to do this is to *write* the objective as well as the "road map" to be followed to reach it—a step-by-step meeting plan to chart the course. Without such a guide, whether written or simply thought out in advance, the chances of reaching the objective are slight indeed.

Imparts Information

When there is pertinent information that is not already known by the group, the leader or some other qualified resource person must supply it. Otherwise the conferees are in the dark and there is no way to stimulate meaningful discussion.

Encourages Discussion

Free and open discussion by an informed group under your leadership is your pathway to a group sale. To achieve this you must do more than simply say, "Now let's have your ideas." Encouraging discussion begins with the kind of atmosphere you create when the conference opens, the invitations you give to participate, and the reception and recognition you give the conferees when they make contributions.

Guides to a Proper Conclusion

This is another way to say, "achieves the conference objective or makes the sale." When the members of the group contribute to the conclusion, they have a proprietary interest in it and support it. As conference leader you must be sensitive to the ideas and the feelings expressed by the group, and flexible enough to reset the objective where this is necessary to reach a proper conclusion.

QUESTIONS ARE THE MASTER KEY

Questions are the master key to successful group leadership. Expertly used, questions help you guide the conference in the direction it should go and at the same time encourage the conferees to do the thinking and the talking.

As leader, you make it a point not to answer questions yourself—instead, you throw them to the group to answer. You use questions to prevent prolonged discussion of side issues and to avert arguments. And you frame questions which form steppingstones to the predetermined objective of the conference.

GUIDELINES TO EFFECTIVE LISTENING

Another important aspect of effective questioning is effective listening. The following guidelines may help you perfect the art of effective listening.

Don't Prejudge

Keep your mind open to any and all comments made by the conferees. Don't jump to conclusions or make up your mind before a conferee has completed a point. Think it through from *his or her point of view*. Ask yourself the question, "What does this really mean to the conferee?"

Try to Understand

Hold yourself and your own preconceived notions in control. Concentrate on understanding not only the *ideas* the conferee expresses, but the *feelings* that lie behind the words.

Use a reentry question like, "Why do you feel that way about it?" or "What have been your experiences on this?" to make sure you understand what he or she means and feels.

Play It Back

To avoid being trapped in a situation in which you think you understand but you really don't, restate the idea the way you understand it, and ask if this is what the conferee really means.

When you plan a conference, chances are it will be, to some degree, a guided conference. If, when you write your conference plan, you find that you have a predetermined objective and that your goal is to win acceptance or enlist support, you *are* planning a guided conference—and your purpose as conference leader, is to *make a sale*.

QUESTION 2
WHY IS PARTICIPATION IMPORTANT IN A CONFERENCE? WHY NOT SIMPLY STATE FACTS CLEARLY AND SAVE TIME AND TROUBLE?

There are times when participation is not only undesirable but impractical. Let's say you call a conference to announce the appointment of a new department manager and explain his or her new duties. You and the new manager are the only ones who have the information. Obviously, participation is impossible until after the announcement.

Or let's say an immediate decision is needed. As conference leader, you must make the decision and communicate it directly to the group for action. To carry this to an extreme, let's say a fire breaks out down the hall. You call your firefighters together and give each one telegraphic instructions. There is no time for discussion *before* they put out the fire. Sometimes the time for participation is not *during* the conference, but *after* it.

- The story is told of a Quaker meeting that was being conducted in traditional silence. Not a word was said for nearly an hour. Finally a non-Quaker guest whispered to

9

his host, "When does the service begin?" The host replied, "Service begins when the meeting is over."

Generally, though, it is the other way around. To get the kind of action you want *after* the conference, you need enthusiastic participation from as many conferees as possible as early as possible. There are good reasons for this, as explained in the following.

"LISTEN TO ME"

People love to express their own ideas. However fascinating your presentation may be, the odds are that at least half the members of your group are sitting on the edge of their seats and "can hardly wait" to give you the benefit of their ideas.

When you encourage your group to participate, you relieve this "Listen to me!" pressure and you gain insights about what the conferees are thinking and feeling that you can get in no other way. There is something about the dynamics of group interaction which reveals inner feelings, and refines and defines ideas more accurately than can be achieved in person-to-person conversation.

Not only can you test what the members of the group have learned but, if you listen perceptively, you can hear more than the words they are saying. You can gauge with surprising accuracy how they *react* to what they have learned.

INSURANCE FOR ACTION

Paul Pigors* has pointed out that when managers consult with their people before making a decision, they benefit in two ways. First, an idea may be expressed in a new, different, and enlightening way. Second, when the employees participate, they are more likely to take action because at least a part of the idea is theirs. The same is true when the members of a conference participate in the discussion—a part of the total product is theirs. This is the best insurance you can hope for in getting action on the idea, the problem, or the project you are considering.

*Paul Pigors, 1949. *Effective Communication in Industry.* New York: National Association of Manufacturers, p. 4.

"WHEN YOU SHARE, YOU CARE"

Closely related to action insurance, and a basic reason for it, is the fact that when you identify yourself with any idea or proposal you adopt it as part of yourself. J. Donald Phillips of Hillsdale College, a lifetime student of communication and participative management, expresses the result of genuine participation in the phrase, "When you share, you care."[*] In an address, Dr. Phillips quoted the sayings, "He who maps the trip enjoys it most," and "He who cuts wood warms himself twice," as other ways of saying "When you share, you care."

---

[*] J. Donald Phillips, former president of Hillsdale College, unpublished addresses.

QUESTION 3
HOW MUCH PRESENTATION AND HOW MUCH PARTICIPATION SHOULD THERE BE IN A GUIDED CONFERENCE?

When you plan a conference, ask yourself, "How much does the group already know about the subject we will be discussing?" The answer will tell you how much new information the group members will need before they can make meaningful contributions, and from this, what the "mix" of presentation and participation should be.

When the group already has a thorough background of knowledge, you can introduce the subject briefly, comment on new aspects that may not be known to the group, and then throw out the first question for discussion.

In other cases in which the group is not familiar with the subject, or in which a number of the conferees are new to the field, you should present the subject in enough detail that everyone can start off properly prepared. As the conference progresses, you can feed in more information to stimulate interest and broaden the base for discussion.

Giving too lengthy or elaborate a presentation to a group that is already well informed, or *feels* that it is, leads only to

13

boredom and lack of interest. On the other hand, not providing enough information results in uncertainty and confusion.
In either case participation suffers.

EXAMPLES OF PRESENTATION–PARTICIPATION MIX

Let's consider examples of conferences in which different
mixes of participation and presentation were used. In the first
case a substantial amount of presentation was needed before
the conferees could make a meaningful contribution.

> The sales manager of a machine tool company called the
> sales staff together for a series of conferences to intro-
> duce a sales technique called "proposal selling."
> The experience of the group ranged from two to
> twenty years and represented an invaluable bank of
> knowledge and skill. Even without knowledge of the
> proposal selling system, this backlog of knowledge made
> it possible to develop active and interested participation.
> After getting basic agreement that more and better
> selling was needed, the conference leader presented the
> new approach in detail. To be sure that every partici-
> pant understood the principles involved, the leader out-
> lined the plan point by point, tying each point to the
> experience of the group and reinforcing each with vi-
> suals.
> The leader gave examples of conventional but un-
> successful presentation, and encouraged the group to
> analyze the reasons for their failure. Then the leader
> gave examples of successful proposal selling approaches,
> and again asked the group to discuss the differences,
> with emphasis on the reasons why the proposal selling
> system led to a completed sale.
> As the conference developed, it became increas-
> ingly participative. Divided into small working groups,
> the members developed their own sales proposals using
> the new procedure. The conference concluded with on-
> the-job work assignments to make sure the newly ac-
> quired technique would be applied when they returned
> to their territories.

Now let's consider a conference in which little, if any, presentation was needed:

> One of the responsibilities of the sales representatives of some petroleum marketers is to recommend locations for new service stations.
>
> Not long ago a major petroleum company held a series of conferences on this important subject. Prior to the conferences, each person received a copy of a new real estate selection manual, which incorporated all the basic information needed. They had an opportunity to read it over and prepare questions on it before they came in for the meeting.
>
> After a few introductory words, the leader opened the meeting with an invitation to "start the questions" and the conference was off to a good start in no time at all. The leader was careful not to answer the questions but referred the conferees to the manual and to their own experience.
>
> By the time the conference was over, everyone knew what the manual contained and how to make best use of the information.

PARTICIPATIVE PRESENTATION

Even when a considerable amount of presentation is needed, it can often be done participatively. As conference leader, you can establish a permissive climate by the way you present your information. Often this climate can be created simply by the way you address the group. You invite ideas from them. You let them know that questions are welcome. You address questions to them if only for a quick nod or comment of agreement. Questions like, "Does your experience check with this?" or "Do you agree?" go a long way toward establishing a feeling of participation.

INVITING PARTICIPATION

A longtime business associate of mine is a master at using the power of participation in conference leadership. He was born in Spain and spent some of his early years there, and in later life he has revisited the Iberian peninsula many times. To show how effective a truly participative lecture can be—and how welcome to the group—he often begins a lecture on Spain by inviting members of the group to draw a map of Spain on a chart pad or chalkboard. This gets the ball rolling. The group members are intrigued by how much or how little they know about the subject. When the map is drawn in recognizable form, he asks the conferees to locate the Pyrenees, the French border, the various oceans and bays—and even the tiny Republic of Andorra, which lies tucked away between Spain and France. In this way, the groundwork is laid for a delightful discussion of Spain spiced with the speaker's personal knowledge of the subject.

If this can be done with a faraway subject like Spain, what an opportunity there is to share experiences on a wide range of conference subjects, from personnel selection to marketing by computer, when the conferees have a direct personal interest in the subject.

PRESENTATION-PARTICIPATION—A CONTINUUM

The mix of the guided conference is on a continuum running from total presentation to total participation. As we have seen, one of the controlling factors in the mix is how much the participants know about the subject as they go into the conference. This implies that the conference leader should *know* how much the group knows and should measure that knowledge *before* making the presentation as well as periodically *during* the presentation. Much can be done in advance of the conference to determine at what point the mixture of presentation and participation will best fit the needs of the group and the target of the session.

Once the group is assembled, and you are in your role as conference leader, you control the blend of the mix. This is a delicate task that requires mastery of the art of questioning and keen sensitivity to the answers and their implications.

QUESTION 4
WHAT IS THE BEST WAY TO GET A CONFERENCE OFF THE GROUND AND ENSURE PLENTY OF PARTICIPATION?

Have you ever faced a conference group and felt as though all the members were *daring* you to make them participate?

If so, you have had an experience common to all conference leaders. Fortunately, however, the members of the group are seldom as forbidding or uncooperative as they seem to be.

As conference leader, it is your job to break through the initial ice of reluctance. There is no single best way to do this, but there are some practical ways to get your conference off to a good start.

FIRST, BE PREPARED

Be sure that you have made your preparations and are ready and relaxed when the conferees begin to arrive. Nothing is more obvious than a leader who nervously fumbles with notes or visual aids as the people begin to arrive for the conference.

17

And nothing throws cold water on the proceedings so fast as a tense and nervous leader. On the other hand, nothing encourages relaxation so much as being relaxed.

Have you ever attended a conference in which the leader was so busy arranging papers and checking last-minute details that he or she didn't have time to look up? What was your reaction? Did you feel like sitting down and joining in an open discussion? Or did you have misgivings about the meeting before it even got under way?

GREET THE CONFEREES

When you have taken the time to make your arrangements and compose yourself before the conference opens, you are in the right frame of mind to greet each person individually and make each feel at home. People like to be introduced to each other and to know each other by name. Then their talking muscles loosen up and they enjoy exchanging ideas.

Some years ago I conducted a conference at the University of Wisconsin with a group of purchasing agents from all over the state. My experience had been limited to facing one purchasing agent at a time—but a whole room full of them!—it was a frightening thought.

One agent came into the conference room with a stormy look, withdrew to the farthest corner, sat down and buried himself in the conference program.

I thought to myself, "There's a tough one. If the rest are like him, it'll be a rough day."

Then a happy thought came. I walked over and introduced myself. He lit up like the sun coming from behind a cloud. And he became one of the most active participants in the day-long conference.

MAKE EVERY INDIVIDUAL FEEL IMPORTANT

People like to feel that what they have to contribute is important to the leader and to the group. When you open the conference—and as you move ahead with it—show by *what you*

do as well as *what you say* that you are glad to be working with *these people* and that every idea they contribute will be welcome.

Even so-called silly ideas should be treated with respect. They may not be as silly as they seem. As S.I. Hayakawa expressed it in *Language in Thought and Action,* * "Let us then silently grant a *tentative* truth value of at least one percent to the person who is speaking, and say to him, 'Tell me more'." Let us not crack down on anyone or poke fun at a person for any idea or question he or she may express.

Remember, your first job as a conference leader is to project the image of friendliness to the group.

INTRODUCE EVERYONE

When your conference is of average size—let's say ten or twenty people—make sure everyone knows everyone else. If you are not known to the group, begin by announcing your name and business connection and write them on a chart pad or chalkboard. Then ask each conferee to introduce himself or herself "loud and clear" so everyone in the room can hear. Have an early coffee break during which you can circulate among the group and make sure everyone knows everyone else.

It also helps everyone present to use "tent" cards with names or nicknames as well as surnames printed on them in heavy black crayon or marker pen. Once the name cards are prepared, use them as much as you can and have the conferees use them. The feeling of knowing each other is a great stimulus to participation.

MAKE IT CLEAR WHAT THE CONFERENCE IS ALL ABOUT

Nothing is more bewildering than to sit in a conference and wonder who called it, why it was called, and what it is all about. Sometimes you wonder whether you are in the right

---

*S.I. Hayakawa, 1949. *Language in Thought and Action*. New York: Harcourt, Brace, p. 238.

meeting. Active participation cannot grow and prosper in a climate of doubt and uncertainty.

A good illustration of this kind of uncertainty occurred at a conference of district managers of one of the principal rubber companies. After the conference had been going for an hour or so, the conference leader, who was the sales manager, interrupted his remarks and walked around to one of the people sitting at the conference table. After a whispered conversation the poor man got up and left the meeting in confusion. He had thought he was in a meeting of the Tire and Rim Association!

LAY OUT CLEAR GROUND RULES

In your opening comments, relieve any personal tensions which may be on the "hidden agenda" of the group. Whether the conference is to be for two hours or two days, each conferee will be thinking about his or her own problems—for example, "When will this conference be over so I can make that important call?"

Tell the group at the outset what the conference plans are, when any breaks will occur, what luncheon or dinner plans may be, and when the conference will close.

If conferees may be receiving messages, tell them how these will be handled—and be sure to let them know where the restrooms are located. When travel arrangements are involved, be sure that everyone knows what is to be done about return reservations.

MAKE A PREMEETING ASSIGNMENT

Whether the conference is to be for only an hour or two or for several days, it often helps to give the group an assignment to work on before they come. When this is done, you have a built-in mutual starting point.

When you have made an advance assignment, be sure that you provide time early in the meeting for the group to discuss it. Don't hold it back, because if you start discussing another subject, your conferees are likely to be concentrating on the assigned problem rather than paying attention to the subject you are discussing.

USE QUESTIONS EARLY IN THE MEETING

Try to keep your opening statements about the meeting as brief as possible. Then throw out a question or two to the group—preferably based on the premeeting assignment. This gets them into a participating mood early in the conference and sets the atmosphere for the rest of the session.

Usually a question addressed to the group as a whole is best at this early stage. A question like, "Who would like to lead off the discussion of the assignment?" may be all that is needed to get the ice broken and the discussion underway. Then by skillful use of follow-up questions, and by practicing the fine art of perceptive listening, you can keep the participation going.

"THIS IS YOUR MEETING"

Summing it all up, the best way to get the meeting off the ground and to ensure plenty of participation is to make every conferee feel at home—to let the group members know that they are invited and expected to share their ideas, and that you mean it when you say, "This is *your* meeting!"

QUESTION 5

WHAT ARE THE PRINCIPAL TYPES OF QUESTIONS TO USE TO GET PARTICIPATION, AND HOW CAN YOU SELECT THE RIGHT TYPES TO ACCOMPLISH YOUR OBJECTIVE?*

The question is a tool, probably the most commonly used tool in the conference leader's kit. Like all tools, however, it can be used skillfully or clumsily, appropriately or inappropriately, effectively or ineffectively, successfully or disastrously.

Questions may be classified in a number of ways. Here we'll consider them according to the *person(s) to whom the question is directed*, the *purpose of the question*, and the *kind of answer it will stimulate*.

PERSON(S) TO WHOM THE QUESTION IS DIRECTED

Here the conference leader has two choices: address the question to an individual conferee using the *direct* or "rifle" type

*The response to this question was written by James P. Dee, Ph.D., Chief, Field Operations Unit, Training Section, United Nations Industrial Development Organization (UNID), formerly Director of Management Development and Education, Ingersoll-Rand, and Professor of Industrial Communication, Bowling Green University.

question; or address the question to all conferees as a group, using the *overhead* or "shotgun" type *question.*

The *direct question* should be used only when the conference leader is sure that the person to whom the question is directed has an answer at his or her finger tips. Otherwise the leader runs the risk of embarrassing the individual and perhaps even "losing" the individual for the rest of the conference. Because it puts the individual on the spot, the direct question may be resented. This is especially true if the conferee happens to be naturally shy or withdrawn, or if his or her thoughts have momentarily wandered.

The best way to avoid these dangers is to precede the question with some kind of warning or notice like, "Jane, how would your department feel about Bill's suggestion of bringing the sales force into the project development group from the very beginning?" By leading off with Jane's name, you alert her that you are going to toss the ball to her, and by restating Bill's suggestion you brief him on the subject of the question.

The *overhead question* should be used when you don't know who has the answer or when you want the group, rather than yourself, to initiate the discussion. Its greatest disadvantage is that it often leads to a "pregnant pause" during which each participant waits for someone else to answer. This pause can be uncomfortable, even frightening, and the temptation to step in with the answer or with another direct question can be great indeed. But the pressure is also on the members of the group to break the silence, and if you can resist the temptation to step in, the overhead question can be an effective discussion-provoking tool.

These two forms of questions may also be used by the conference leader to handle questions from the participants. Usually it is advisable for the leader *not* to answer such questions, but to draw the answers from the group. This is especially true in the early minutes of the conference, when the tone of the entire discussion is established. When a participant addresses a question to the leader, the leader should bounce the question back to the questioner (a "recoil" question), to another member of the group (a "ricochet" question), or to all the conferees as a *redirected overhead* question.

PURPOSE OF THE QUESTION

Unless they are rhetorical, all questions are intended to evoke a response. But it might be helpful to remember that there are many kinds of responses. For example, you might be seeking a *factual* response—to elicit facts, data, information. Or your purpose may be to *provoke discussion*—to incite the conferees to answer, or to elicit personal or expert opinion. Factual and provocative questions are probably the basic classifications, but your questions can serve many other purposes, for instance:

- To serve as a transition to another phase of the discussion.
- To direct attention to a point not yet considered by the group.
- To direct attention to difficulties or complexities so far undetected by the conferees.
- To register steps of agreement.
- To point up areas of disagreement.

The list is almost endless. If you are aware of your purpose in asking a question, you are in a better position to achieve that purpose effectively.

KIND OF ANSWER STIMULATED

Questions classified by the kind of answer stimulated fall into these major categories: the *yes–no* question, the *who-what-when-where-how-why* question, and the *leading* question.

Effective conference leaders generally avoid questions that lead to a yes or no answer. There is a finality to this kind of reply that tends to shut off discussion, or at least to dampen the conference atmosphere. The conference leader (or *any* questioner) is seldom looking for such a response and consequently the yes–no reply is likely to be inadequate, incomplete, and unenlightening. When you do find it necessary to use this type of question, be sure to follow it up immediately with the reentry or "depth bomb" question, "Why?"

The who-what-when-where-how-why type of question is generally preferable to the yes–no question. It is provocative.

It incites or stimulates fuller and more complete answers. This type of question is more likely to produce the kind of answer being sought, and it encourages other participants to speak up, to "hitchhike" on the reply.

The leading question is often frowned on in our society, undeservedly so. Whether it is good or bad, ethical or unethical, depends on the purpose for which it is used. Leading questions are quite legitimate in conference leadership when, for example, they are used to:

- Suggest the answer desired.

- Suggest alternatives from which a desired answer may be selected.

- Suggest that we don't have all available or necessary information.

- Suggest that the group is in agreement on the point and that the discussion should now move on to the next point.

Again, the list is almost endless. The value of the leading question is that, with its use, the conference leader *invites* the group to make its own decision on the question rather than *imposing* his or her own answer on the group. One of the classic leading questions of all time was, "What profiteth it a man if he gain the whole world and lose his own soul?"

It has been the purpose of this chapter to point up the many ways of looking at *the question*—the most commonly used and most versatile tool in the conference leader's kit. Hopefully, the more aware we are of the tools available, and how to use them, the more expertly and effectively we can put them to work.

SUMMARY

QUESTIONS: CLASSIFICATION OF TYPES

Person(s) to whom question is directed	Purpose of question	Kind of answers stimulated
1. Direct—to one conferee (Rifle)	Basic types 1. Factual—requests an answer; seeks to elicit facts, data, information	1. Yes–No Avoid in general When used, follow up with question "Why?"
2. Overhead—to all conferees; anyone answers (Shotgun)	2. Provocative—incites to answer; seeks to elicit opinion, personal or expert	
3. Redirected—question put by conferee to leader is bounced back (Ricochet or recoil)	Additional purposes 1. To serve as transition to another phase	2. Who-what-when-where-how-why Prefer this type
a) Redirected–Direct—to one conferee; perhaps to the conferee who posed it (recoil)	2. To emphasize a point which has been made 3. To direct attention to a point not yet raised	Calls for explanation, stimulates discussion
b) Redirected–Overhead—to all conferees	4. To direct attention to difficulties or complexities undetected by the conferees	3. Leading
	5. To direct attention to the source of a fact or opinion, of information or argument	Suggests the answer desired, or perhaps alternatives from which a desired answer may be selected
	6. To determine how strong an argument really is	
	7. To suggest that we don't have all available or necessary information	
	8. To suggest that group is on a tangent	
	9. To register steps of agreement	
	10. To point up areas of disagreement	

SUMMARY (Cont.)

11. To suggest that the group is not ready to take action

12. Where two clear-cut, equally strong factions exist, to suggest that a compromise be sought

13. To suggest that nothing will be gained by further delay

14. To suggest that some conferees are talking too much or too little

15. To suggest that personal remarks be avoided

16. To suggest that conferees may be prejudiced

QUESTION 6

HOW DO YOU LOOSEN UP A CONFERENCE WHEN THE MEMBERS DON'T SEEM TO WANT TO RESPOND?

You have opened the conference, made everyone feel welcome, and stated the purpose of the conference as clearly as you know how. Then you throw out a shotgun or overhead question—and the group just sits there. What's the trouble and what can you do about it?

ARE YOU ON THE SAME WAVELENGTH?

This is the point at which all your advance planning pays off. You know what your objective is and you have a plan for achieving it.

But how about the members of your group? Is it possible that they are sitting there wondering what you are really trying to accomplish? Are they asking themselves, "What am I expected to do about it?" or "What does this conference mean to me?"

The fact may be that you are on one mental wavelength and the members of the group are on another. This is one of the reasons why it may help to have a premeeting work assignment. With such an assignment, you always have a beginning point that makes sense to both leader and conferees.

When there has been no advance assignment, it is important that you *find* a beginning point that makes sense to the members of the group and, at the same time, makes it possible for them to get tuned in not only to the subject matter but also to the general idea behind the conference.

> At a conference of branch managers of a metropolitan bank, the conference leader, who was known and respected by them all, couldn't seem to get meaningful responses to his questions. When he addressed a question to an individual, the response was brief and not meaningful. Finally, he made a flat statement which he knew that 90 percent of the managers would disagree with—and threw the subject open for discussion. It was like opening a dike. Discussion came in a rush.

HAVE YOU READ YOUR GROUP RIGHT?

As you face the group, it may seem to you that they express by their silence an *unwillingness* to cooperate. Is this the right reading? Are they really unwilling? Or is their silence expressing puzzlement or uncertainty? Are they simply taking the time required to think through the purpose you have expressed or the question you have asked?

How often have you been mistaken when you tried to size up another person's reaction by the facial expression alone? If you are like most people, you are likely to be wrong more often than you are right. And the problem is ten times as difficult when you have ten people together for a conference.

In my early school days, I was sitting at my desk one morning feeling dejected and trying my best to look pitiful. While I was concentrating on my facial expression, the teacher strode over and shook me up for "looking insolent." How wrong one can be!

THE STRATEGIC WAIT

Let's say that you have briefly explained a new company procedure and have asked a shotgun question like this:

> "How do you feel you can best follow through on this new procedure?"

The question is greeted with silence. Some members of the group seem more interested in the outside landscape than in concentrating on the question. Some don't seem to be thinking at all, and others just look at you. What's the trouble?

More likely than not, there is no trouble at all. It takes time to ingest the question, still more time to digest it, and again more time to put one's ideas together and then put them into words. Dr. Edgar Dale, Professor Emeritus, The Ohio State University, calls this silent period "the strategic wait" and points out that it is a necessary part of the participative process.* Often the wait seems endless, but it is usually only a few seconds. Try this: Ask someone else to keep time for you. Ask a question and think about the answer for *10 seconds.* How long that 10 seconds can seem!

Wait it out. Give the mental machinery of the group a chance to get rolling. Chances are that when the mental gears are meshed and the wheels are turning, you will get even more responses than you expect.

BUT IF THERE'S STILL NO RESPONSE—WHAT THEN?

There is an end to your patience, and you finally decide that something has to be done to get the group loosened up. What should you do?

Rephrase the Question

Ask the question again, giving it a slightly different twist or slant. Instead of repeating it, rephrase it like this:

> The new procedure calls for followthrough to make sure we get the best possible results. What steps would you take?

---

*Edgar Dale, conversations with the author.

Or you might rephrase the question and suggest a couple of contradictory ways in which it might be answered. Then toss it to the group again.

Use a Direct Question

Address a direct question to one member of the group you feel may be especially well qualified to respond. This is a rifle question rather than a shotgun question. In framing the question, start by identifying the person to whom the question is addressed so he or she can be alerted to pick up the question when it comes along. Using the same question you had asked the group and rephrasing it only slightly, you might say:

> "Pat, you have had a good deal of experience with the old procedure. How would you follow up under this new way of operating?"

AFTER THE BALL GETS ROLLING

Whether you ask a shotgun question or a rifle question, don't settle for the first answer you get, because the chances are that it will be only a partial answer. Certainly you won't get the ideas of all the members of the group.

Use the Reentry Question

Let's say one member has replied that the first step would be to set up a date for a call-back on the account to check the stock. Dig a little deeper with a reentry question like this:

> "Pat, why would that be the first step you would take? What is your reasoning behind this?"

Toss the Ball to Someone Else

With the members of the group on the same wavelength with you and beginning to respond constructively to your questions, there is one important "don't" to keep in mind. Don't yield to the temptation to answer the question yourself. Let the group do it even if you know very well that you are the best-informed person on the subject in the room.

Work with the group by using direct and overhead questions and by tossing the ball to other members for their ideas until you get a satisfactory answer. It may not be expressed in just the words you had hoped to hear, but it is substantially correct. Then you can rephrase the answer to smooth out the rough spots—and get agreement from the group members that this is what they had in mind.

Don't Settle for the "Wrong" Answer

Often there is more than one right answer. But just as often there are many possible wrong answers. These answers may be wrong because they are in conflict with policy or other procedures, or because they are simply not workable. Be sure the answers you develop through responses from the group are good, practical answers within the framework of the policies of your company or organization.

RAPPORT WITH THE GROUP

As the conference moves along, you will develop a sensitivity to the group, and it to you, that will lead to rapport and mutual understanding. This rapport provides the climate for free communication, releases ideas, and stimulates interchange of thoughts among all conference members. When you see an individual who seems to have a glimmer of interest or who indicates that he or she has an idea to express, give some warning and call on him or her for a contribution. The result may not be what you expected, but at least you've created involvement and there will be more willingness to participate as the conference progresses.

7

How many times have you been in a meeting in which it seemed that the chairperson or meeting leader had no really solid ideas of why the meeting was called or what its purpose was?

After an hour of aimless talk, the only option the leader had was to make an arbitrary decision, assume agreement from the group, and bring the meeting to an end.

With a well-planned guided conference, such an unhappy situation can't happen to you for the simple reason that you have put down in black and white what your objective is, and then worked out a step-by-step plan to reach the objective.

YOU NEED A MEETING PLAN

To arrive at your predetermined objective in a guided conference, you need an organized meeting plan. Without it you stand a good chance of getting "lost in the woods" like the unfortunate conference leader mentioned above.

When you try to "fight it out" without a clearly defined plan, as many conference leaders do, you are in much the same position as the vacationer who takes off on a trip without a destination and without a road map. Every side road holds its own temptation and the choice of which way to go must be whimsical and arbitrary. The net result may be that the traveler winds up face to face with a "Dead End" sign. It's much the same in controlling the direction of a guided conference.

Prepare the Plan in Writing

It's usually best to prepare the meeting plan in writing, especially if there are several major points to be made. Your plan should include a simple, straightforward statement of the conference objective. It should also include all the key questions you plan to ask the conferees to guide their thoughts. The questions should be developed and arranged in sequence so that they lead logically to the objective you have selected.

Assuming, then, that the answers from the group will lead to a conclusion you consider proper, plan a brief summary statement and, if appropriate, an assignment to be given to the group before adjournment.

Be Prepared for a Change of Direction

Without a meeting plan designed along the lines suggested, your chances of reaching your conference destination are slim unless you arbitrarily take over from the group. Even with a well-worked-out conference plan you still must be prepared to modify your objective, or even change your sales plan, depending on the reaction you get from your group. Certainly you cannot expect them simply to accept your viewpoint or automatically rubberstamp the decision contained in your conference plan.

The real point, of course, is that when you have a sound, well-worked-out plan for the conference you know where you are headed. Consequently you can use your questions effectively to guide the group to an acceptable conclusion. At no time is it necessary to impose your views or your preferences on the conference group.

A SUGGESTED CONFERENCE OUTLINE

The outline for a one- or two-hour conference on time management might look something like this:

Objective

To develop a workable plan to enable these managers to spend more time working with their salespeople.

Questions

1. What percent of your time do you figure you now spend in routine office work? How much in direct sales work with your salespeople in the field? How do you know this?

2. How much of your time do you feel you should be spending with your salespeople?

3. What steps can you take to make more of your time available for work with your salespeople?

4. What activities are now demanding most of your time? How much of an average day or week does each consume? To what degree can you control these demands?

5. If you suddenly found that you had three extra 8-hour days available for work during the month, how would you spend them?

Summary

More time is spent in general office duties than we would like to believe. It is important to concentrate on doing the things that will lead to increased business. This includes spending more time with the salespeople.

Assignment

Take a week between now and the next meeting to maintain a time tally of how you spend each 15-minute segment of each day. Study the tally and be prepared to report your findings at the next meeting.

FRAME THE BASIC QUESTIONS

As shown in the suggested conference plan, you should frame in advance the questions you plan to ask. Your questions can and will be tempered by developments in the conference, but at least you will have a clear idea of the direction you plan to take, the road map you plan to follow.

FRAME THE ANSWERS, TOO

Probably one of the main reasons why so many guided (or misguided) conferences wind up in confusion and indecision is that the leader hasn't done enough homework. It is vitally important that you think through each of your key questions before the conference and determine what you believe an acceptable answer should be. To do this you may want to consult with other staff members before the conference.

This does not mean that you will *receive* answers that coincide with those you have written down. It does mean, however, that you will have a clear idea of what an adequate answer is and will be able to conduct the discussion accordingly.

When you write down the acceptable answers before the conference, it does not mean that you are trying to influence the answers from the group. On the contrary, properly used, these prepared answers will make it possible for you to consider carefully the answers from the conferees and, through the process of questioning, to arrive at conclusions that accurately reflect the group judgment.

TO SUM IT UP

When you *write down* a clear idea of your conference objectives and your plan of approach to them, and when you use questions effectively and flexibly, always resisting the temptation to answer them yourself, you'll keep the conference on its course—and you will not dominate. You won't have to.

QUESTION **8**

HOW DO YOU WORK WITH A
GROUP WITH MIXED EXPERIENCE
AND STILL MAINTAIN INTEREST?

Often a mixed group provides a better opportunity for an exciting and productive conference than a group in which all the conferees have the same level of knowledge and experience. With different viewpoints and backgrounds represented, many different aspects of the subject can be explored.

The secret is to find the subject areas that make most sense to the group and that spark interest and group interaction. The opportunity for a successful conference is there — and so is the challenge.

At a certain American Management Association marketing conference, attendance was so mixed that it seemed next to impossible to discover a common denominator. Some of the conferees were senior executives who had spent many years in marketing. Others were just beginning their first marketing assignment. A subject area that interested some of the newer people was "old hat" to the veterans. Finally the leader touched on a subject

of *mutual* interest—the need for trained supervision—
and from that point on the only problem was to keep
the conference on the track.

FIND OUT HOW "MIXED" YOUR GROUP IS

Every group, however carefully selected, is mixed to some
extent. There are variations in depth of knowledge, years of
experience, and areas of specialization. Some of the conferees
are more interested in one aspect of the subject than others.

As conference leader you should attempt to discover the
common interest that makes the difference between a
"group" and simply a miscellaneous assembly of people. Once
you have done this, you are on your way to a successful conference.

There are many ways to discover this common denominator. One way is the direct approach of putting an overhead
question to the group something like this:

> "The subject we're here to cover today is a broad one
> and one that presents many problems. What phase of
> the subject do you feel is most important to you?"

THEN USE THE CHART PAD OR THE CHALKBOARD

Don't expect to have immediate agreement from every member of the group. Write on the chart pad or chalkboard every
idea you can pull from the group. Don't settle for the first
few that are expressed. Do your best to see that everyone
makes a contribution.

If some of the responses seem to overlap others already
charted, write them down anyway. This encourages everyone
to participate. Duplicates can easily be eliminated later. And
don't attempt to grade or rank the responses until everyone
has been heard from. Then check the ones in which the group
has the greatest interest and decide on a starting point.

With this kind of participation, the old and the new
members, experienced and inexperienced, will be involved to
a point where the "mix" will be a benefit rather than a
handicap.

PUT EXPERIENCE TO WORK

As the conference progresses, you will find that some members know a good deal about the subject. Use them. Invite them to share with the newer members the experience they have built up over the years. Don't expect the younger members to accept automatically the wisdom of the veterans. Encourage them to question or challenge any viewpoints they feel need clarification or modification.

QUESTIONS ARE THE ANSWER

When one of the senior members has made a contribution, throw a shotgun question to the group. See how the idea is accepted by others and follow up with the all-important re-entry question: "Tell us more—why do you feel that way?"

With members of the group reacting to the problem, ask direct, or rifle, questions of some of the younger members. Get the benefit of their ideas. Depending upon the group's and your own interest, toss the question back to one of the more experienced members so that everyone becomes actively involved.

This kind of free-wheeling discussion makes is possible to cross-fertilize the thoughts of the newer conferees with those of the experienced ones. It can also cause experienced members to reexamine their own ideas. The result will be the development and clarification of ideas through group interaction, which would not have happened otherwise.

MAKE USE OF RESOURCES

Where you have the opportunity to talk to members of the group in advance, it is often a good idea to ask some of the more experienced people for their help as resource persons. Let them know that you will be looking to them for ideas on specialized phases of the subject. You may want to plant specific questions with these senior members and ask that they be ready to respond. Be sure to stress the point that the question will be asked of them without any special introduction and that it should be handled as briefly as possible. Otherwise this plan may backfire as it did at a conference on industrial lubricants some years ago.

> The subject was a highly technical one on which several of the old-timers present were recognized experts. The conference leader had arranged in advance with three of these members to respond to questions on the subject of viscosity in lubricating oils. The conference started off with brisk participation and continued that way until one of the experts was called on for ideas. At this point the expert took over the conference, turned it into a lecture, and there was no time, opportunity, or inclination for participation by the other conferees.

It's great to have experts who are willing to act as resource people. But it's important that they understand in advance that they are to keep their comments brief and not yield to the temptation to show their depth of knowledge by taking over the conference.

BLENDING OF INTERESTS

With a mixed group with different levels of knowledge, age, sex, and experience, it is possible to blend the interests of all. The sooner you discover the true mix of the group, the more opportunity you will have to stir the mixture into an exciting and stimulating exchange of ideas. But make sure you have assayed the group composition accurately. Otherwise, instead of a conference, you may wind up with a tug-of-war.

QUESTION 9

HOW CAN THE CONFERENCE LEADER TAKE THE TEMPERATURE OF THE GROUP?

There are many ways to "take the temperature" of a conference group—to make sure that the members' interest has not cooled, and that you are getting through to them effectively.

TUNE IN TO THE GROUP

To change metaphors for a moment, probably the most effective way to be sure interest is being maintained is to keep "tuned in" to the group as the conference progresses. This is a difficult process to describe and even more difficult to do. It can be summed up in the word "sensitivity," which is probably the single most important attribute of successful conference leaders. It is the ability to note and correctly interpret the reactions of the group without pressing or asking direct questions. It is a sixth sense—and it comes only through experience.

If you sense a feeling of boredom, indicated by an uneasy shifting of position or a noticeable reduction in participation, you are getting a signal that the message of the conference is not getting through. The reason may be that the subjects being discussed don't interest the group or that the conferees don't have enough information on the subject to make intelligent contributions. In either case, they lose interest.

What's Wrong?

Before the conference can be made fully effective it is necessary to find out *why* the group has lost interest. Until this is done, the temperature of the group will continue to drop until all interest may disappear.

TAKE THE TEMPERATURE WITH A SHOTGUN QUESTION

The most direct, and perhaps the simplest way to measure interest is to use a shotgun question. Simply ask the group, "Does this subject interest you?" or "How do you feel about this? Are we on the right track?" or "How about it? Are we making sense?"

This may seem like a hammer-and-tongs way to go after the problem, but it often gives a fairly accurate reading on how the group feels and helps determine whether a new problem or a new approach should be introduced.

You may find, for example, that you have been doing too much talking and have not let the group participate enough. Or the opposite may be true. You may be expecting the group to enter actively into a discussion when they don't feel they have enough information or experience to contribute.

QUESTION KEY PEOPLE

Another way to take the temperature is to toss a question to one or two key people. Ask a question like, "Claire, how do you feel about the progress we have made so far? Are we working out answers that are helpful to you?"

And don't settle for a single answer. Relay the questions to another of your key participants and make sure the direction you are taking is the best one for this group at this particular time.

At break time, when you get an opportunity, circulate among the various groups who are having coffee or a smoke together. Ask them, frankly, "How do you feel we are doing?" "So far have we helped you with the problem we're here to discuss?" "Any suggestions on how we can pin the discussion down to more practical points?"

HAVE AN OBSERVER

It is sometimes possible to have an observer or co-worker sitting in the conference who can give you the benefits of his or her reactions and pass on tips which come from observation of the group. Such an observer can be of special usefulness if he or she knows both the conferees and the subject being discussed. Check at every opportunity and ask the question, "How are we doing?" Then *listen* to the response—and make the necessary changes.

USE A WRITTEN TALLY

Some conference leaders make it a point to pass a small slip of paper to each person once or twice during each conference session and ask for a quick written answer to the question, "So far do you feel that this conference has been beneficial to you?"

At the close of the conference, or perhaps after a half-day of work, you may find it useful to ask questions such as:

- So far, what do you like most about this conference?
- What do you like least about this conference?
- Check how you would rate the conference:
  Excellent ___ Good ___ Fair ___ Poor ___

AFTER THE CONFERENCE

After the conferees have returned home and had a chance to think over the benefits of the conference, write them and ask for their answers to the same questions. It may also be helpful to ask for specific comments on what should be omitted and what should be added in forthcoming conferences. Although these comments are of no use in the conference just completed, they can help greatly in planning the next one.

THE BEST THERMOMETER

All the methods we have discussed are useful in getting an on-the-spot reading of the temperature of the group. But best of all is the reading from your own senses of how the group really feels. Their reactions to your questions, their willingness to commit themselves in their responses, the nature and direction of their comments, will all give you an accurate gauge of the progress you are making toward your conference objective.

10

HOW CAN THE CONFERENCE LEADER DETERMINE WHETHER THE PRESENTATION IS IN LINE WITH THE KNOWLEDGE, CAPACITY, AND INTEREST LEVELS OF THE GROUP?

Your success as a conference leader depends more on how well you know your group and the skills of conference leadership than on how well you know the subject matter. A resource person can help with the technical information, but only you can feel the pulse of the group.

Some knowledge and feeling for the group can be acquired before the conference, some can be learned during the conference, and some may come only after it is over.

WHAT YOU CAN LEARN BEFORE THE CONFERENCE

Although on a rare occasion you may have no way to get advance information about the conferees, more often than not you will have the opportunity to learn something about their individual backgrounds.

Study the experience of each member. Is he or she new to the company? New on the job? Has he or she had similar experiences elsewhere? Do you have any mutual experiences

51

or associations? Are there any "old hands" who can be relied on to give sound, thoughtful responses based on their experience? Are there any mavericks who can be expected to come up with irrelevant or controversial ideas? What is the mix of the group? Is it made up of some beginners and some veterans? Some successful operators and others who may be marginal or poor? Are there some to whom you can give advance assignments or ask to think about certain aspects of the subject before the conference convenes?

If you don't have the answers to these and other related questions, it is a good idea to search out someone in the organization who does, and review the conference roster with him or her. However you do it, don't overlook the opportunity to get acquainted with your group before the session begins.

WHAT YOU CAN LEARN DURING THE CONFERENCE

You can learn a great deal more about the knowledge and capacity, and particularly the interest, of the group as you lead the conference.

Usually the easiest and most natural approach is to open with a shotgun question that gives all members in the group the opportunity to think the problem over and volunteer their ideas. Often this first overhead question will give you insights into all three subjects—"How much does the group know?" "How much capacity do they have to learn more?" and "How interested are they in the subject?"

As the conference continues, shift to direct questions capitalizing on the interest you see developing in different individuals. When you receive responses from these rifle questions, follow up with reentry or "trigger" questions that dig deeper and probe for real interest in the subject. A typical trigger question is something like this: "What you have said makes a great deal of sense. How did you arrive at this conclusion?" When you are satisfied that you have probed the subject deeply enough with one respondent, pass the question to another member and get a new viewpoint.

Play your questions as you would play the keys of an organ; always select them to develop the harmony or melody,

or even the discords, which are called for in your conference plan.

Dr. Ralph G. Nichols, former head of the Department of Rhetoric at the University of Minnesota and co-author of *Are You Listening?*, has prepared the following list of reasons for asking questions—many of them related to conference situations and the need to understand better the knowledge, capacity, and interest level of the conferees.[*]

- To get information about the other person.
- To get information about the subject.
- To obtain helpful advice, criticism, or suggestions.
- To discover what people in your field want.
- To discover what this person wants.
- To find the weaknesses in your program, plan, or project.
- To suggest alternative plans of action, any of which you like.
- To discover how much the other person knows about the subject.
- To discover the other person's attitude toward the project, plan, program, idea.
- To arouse interest or capture attention.
- To ensure that the other person is still listening (stop and ask a question to keep on the track).
- To encourage the other person to return to the main topic.
- To focus attention on an aspect of the problem not yet considered, or not considered fully.
- To build a "positive response" frame of mind—called the "Yes" technique—usually through leading questions.
- To close the sale, or get the person to say "Yes."
- To get the other person to accept an idea or project (by asking the individual to point out advantages or good points).
- To uncover the other person's motivations.

[*] Lecture notes.

- To get reassurance for yourself that the person is still in agreement, understands so far, etc.
- To get the other person to feel at ease.
- To bolster the other person's ego.
- To prove to the other person that you are listening.
- To enable the other person to prove a point, by asking for specific reasons, illustrations, statistics, and authority.
- To show your understanding of the subject.
- To pass information on to the other person.
- To get the other person to illuminate or develop a point.
- To overcome antagonism (let the person tell you what is wrong and then ask, "What else . . . ?").
- To show you are interested in the individual.
- To avoid having to answer a question (reverse the question).
- To allow yourself time to think.
- To avoid an argument.
- To embarrass the other person.
- To win an argument, by backing the other person into a corner.
- To draw the other person into an argument.
- To make the other person feel ill at ease.
- To get "food" for gossiping about.
- To prove that the other person doesn't know what he or she is talking about.
- To help the other person diagnose his or her own problem.
- To help the other person discover his or her own need for information or assistance.
- To shift the responsibility for problem-solving to another's shoulders.
- To discover what progress has been made already toward the solution of the problem.
- To encourage thinking.

- To encourage the person to become more independent of help.
- To help distinguish between symptoms and the real causes.
- To help discover the importance of the problem and the need for immediate remedial steps.
- To help discover the possible effects of the plan of action being considered.
- To help the person plan how to put the proposed solution into operation.
- To encourage consideration of alternative courses of action.

Checkpoints on Asking and Answering Questions

Dr. Nichols has also compiled a series of checkpoints that can be especially helpful in using questions with conferees:

- Start the questioning with friendly and easily answered questions.
- Plan some of the questions you want to ask, before the meeting.
- Know what you want your question to achieve. Are you asking for or giving information? asking a favor or doing one?
- If you want to draw the other person out, reflect the person's emotional content: "So you think your situation is hopeless?"
- Get a sense of partnership when trying to get facts involving a person's behavior.
- If trying to get the person to talk, avoid questions that solicit a "yes" or "no" answer.
- Statements can also be effective as questioning devices, e.g., "Tell me about . . . ."
- To get personal or difficult information, try the simple trick of overstatement. People like to correct a mistake.

- Avoid getting too personal in your questioning.
- Don't ask questions that you are fairly certain the other person won't be able to answer.
- Be sure to couch your questions in terms the person can understand.
- Allow the person time to think before he or she answers your question.

WHAT YOU CAN LEARN AFTER THE CONFERENCE

Anything you learn after the conference obviously won't help you to make progress during the conference, but it can help you in two other ways: in following through for results, and in preparing for the next conference with this or a similar group.

Following through for Results

Whenever possible, conclude the conference with a work assignment, planned in such a way that you can analyze the results. This will show how well your ideas got through to the group and what additional information is needed.

A simple questionnaire to be completed by each conferee and returned to you will also tell what additional information may be needed. Questions like, "What part of the conference did you feel was most helpful to you?" and "What part of the conference was least helpful?" will help you get accurate reading on follow up that may be needed.

Preparing for the Next Conference

Questionnaires completed while the recollection of the conference is still fresh are also useful in planning the next conference. The question, "What segments of the conference would you omit if you were planning this conference?" and "What subjects would you add that were not included?" provide helpful background as you prepare for the next conference either with the same group or with other groups.

Also, your own reflections on where the group seemed most interested and most responsive, and least interested and least responsive, will provide guidelines for future conference planning.

11

HOW CAN THE CONFERENCE LEADER DETERMINE THE FEELINGS OF THE GROUP MEMBERS AND USE THIS KNOWLEDGE TO REACH THE CONFERENCE OBJECTIVE?

Let's start with the first part of the question.

HOW CAN YOU DETERMINE THE FEELINGS OF THE GROUP MEMBERS?

Whether the group numbers 2 or 20 or 200, *it* does not have feelings. Only the individual members do. However, the total feelings of the group will differ from the simple total of the individual reactions. This synergistic characteristic of a conference group is a kind of "X" factor that results from the effect each person present has on all other members and from the interaction of all the members on each individual.

In some ways the members of a group are more adventurous than they would be as individuals. Membership in a group may reinforce them and give them courage to express their ideas. On the other hand, individuals in a group often have a tendency to be more conservative than they would be in one-to-one communication.

As the thoughts of one individual play on the thoughts of the others, and then in turn are played back in somewhat altered form, new ideas and combinations of ideas are born. This natural inclination to "hitchhike" on other people's ideas is a normal product of group interaction.

As conference leader you must be sensitive to the fact that each conferee is an individual with his or her own feelings and ideas, but that as a member of a group his or her reactions will often differ from what they would be in personal face-to-face conversation. To understand the feelings of a group member, it is necessary to understand not only the member's feelings as an individual, but also the impact of the group on the individual's feelings.

Questions—the Key

Again, plenty of questions and perceptive listening are the key to the problem. Trigger questions that touch off underlying feelings, and filter questions that separate surface feelings from real feelings, are especially useful. Questions like these can often provide insights into what the conferee is really thinking:

> "You've told us that you have some doubts about the plan we've been discussing. As you see it, what are the main problems involved?"

> "Jean, tell us, why do you feel that way about the program?"

> "Why is that?"

> "Will you tell us more about your ideas on this?"

> Or just plain "Why?"

With trigger questions and filter questions like these working for you, the next critical step is to listen "with the other person's ears." Try to understand *what the real meaning is*, by listening between the lines to *what is being said*. The two may be, and probably are, different.

How Many Personalities Are There in the Group?

Dr. Oliver Wendell Holmes, father of the United States Supreme Court Justice, wrote that whenever two people get together there are actually six personalities present. One plus one equals six.* Here's the way the process works:

Tom Meets Jane

Tom's Personalities

- Tom's Tom
  (Tom's idea of himself)
- Jane's Tom
  (Jane's idea of Tom)
- The real Tom

Jane's Personalities

- Jane's Jane
  (Jane's idea of herself)
- Tom's Jane
  (Tom's idea of Jane)
- The real Jane

When Tom meets Jane, he can communicate only with the Jane he knows. The reverse is true when Jane speaks to Tom. Obviously, Tom's concept of himself and Jane's idea of Tom may be poles apart. To complicate matters, often the *real* Tom and the *real* Jane are largely unknown to either of them. It's a complex problem even when *two* individuals meet in face-to-face conversation. How much more complicated it is when 8 or 10 or 20 individuals meet in a group.

So How about Groups?   It's more than a simple arithmetical progression advancing in direct proportion to the number in the group. If it were that simple, 20 people in the group would have 6 personalities each, for a total of 120 personalities.

P (personalities present) $= [N$ (number in the group) $+ 1] N$

But for a conference of 20 people, the formula would work out this way:

$$P = (20 + 1)20$$
Personalities present $= 420$

That's a lot of personalities and creates a lot of problems in communication and understanding.

---

* Dr. Oliver Wendell Holmes, *The Autocrat of the Breakfast Table.* Boston: Phillips, Sampson, 1858, p. 59.

Again, Questions Are the Key!   All you can do is try for as close an understanding of Jane's idea of Jane and Tom's idea of Tom as you possibly can. Through the use of direct questions, reentry questions, ricochet and recoil questions, try to get under the skin and begin to see things from Jane and Tom's points of view—and the points of view of every other conferee.

You have one important advantage going for you. By properly directing your questions, you can listen to what Jane thinks about Tom's ideas and what every other conferee thinks about the ideas and feelings expressed by the other group members. Not only does participation make all group members feel that they are having a part in the proceedings, but it also reveals the thoughts and feelings of the group members for your consideration and analysis.

This interaction, or group process, provides the means to see beneath the surface of superficial comment and gain a "three-dimensional" understanding of real meanings and underlying feelings.

Now for a look at the second part of the question.

HOW CAN YOU USE THIS KNOWLEDGE
TO CARRY YOU TO YOUR OBJECTIVE?

Your conference objective may have been declared, or at this point it may be known fully only to you. The extent of knowledge and acceptance of the objective depends on a number of factors: the nature of the group, the personality and status of the group leader, the nature of the subject, and how far the conference has progressed.

If at this stage, through skillful questioning and sensitive listening, you have arrived at an understanding of the feelings of the group members, you are in a position to move ahead toward your objective.

If you sense that the group members recognize a need that coincides with your conference objective, you are obviously on the way to a successful conclusion. You are ready to develop a solution to that need, show how it works, follow through with the necessary proof, and lead to the action you want.

On the other hand, if you find their thoughts and feelings to be contrary to your objective, you may be faced with the necessity to change your pace, your approach, or even your objective.

Your ability to read accurately the thoughts and feelings of the group is at once the most difficult and the most critical phase of your assignment. The only key that will unlock the feelings of individuals, either as separate personalities or as members of the group, is the question—the way you ask it, the way you listen, the way you respond.

Responding to Questions

Your response to questions can often lead you to your conference objective. Dr. Nichols suggests these four simple steps:

- Repeat the question asked if you don't understand it.
- Don't read into questions meanings that aren't really there.
- Ask a question in return when you want clarification of the meaning or intent of the original question.
- Reverse the question to the original questioner if you feel he or she should accept the responsibility for deciding on the answer.

Whether you are searching out the true feelings of your conferees, or attempting to lead them to acceptance and action on your conference objective, effective questioning and sensitive listening, coupled with satisfying response, are your most versatile tools.

QUESTION 12

HOW CAN THE LEADER AVOID ANSWERING THE GROUP'S QUESTIONS, ESPECIALLY WHEN KNOWING THE ANSWERS BETTER THAN ANYONE ELSE?

More often than not the members of the group look to the conference leader as an authority on the subject being discussed, and naturally look to the leader to supply authoritative answers.

IT'S A MATTER OF POSITION

Your position in the front of the room or at a speaker's table or podium puts you in a spot in which it is natural for the group to defer to your opinion, or at the very least to expect a statement of it in response to questions.

The fact that you have been delegated to be conference leader is another factor that conditions the group to expect definitive answers from you. When, as is often the case, you are also the immediate supervisor of the group, or at least of higher organizational rank, the tendency to look to you for answers is strong indeed.

So Why Not Answer?

Granted, it would be much simpler to answer the group's questions than to attempt to draw the answers from them. Then why not do so?

The reason is simple. The name of the game is *participation* and, if you answer the questions, the session becomes a lecture and the group members don't become personally involved. They will find it easy just to coast along, accept the answers they hear, and possibly drift off into a state of dreamy inaction.

A PLACE FOR PARTICIPATION
AND A PLACE FOR PRESENTATION

Before starting a conference, of course, it is fundamental to determine whether the idea is one which *can* be communicated participatively, or whether it should simply be explained to the group by conventional presentation.

Here is a simple five-point checklist, developed for and by conference leaders, to check out in advance which method or combination of methods should be used:

- *Is the idea sound?*
  If it is not sound, why bother trying to communicate it at all?

- *Can it be communicated?*
  Even if the idea is sound, is it the kind of idea that can be put across to this particular group?

- *Is it worthwhile?*
  It may be possible to put the idea across, but is the objective worth the time, the effort, and the money required to do it in a conference? Would it be better simply to write it up and mail it to the group?

- *Is it timely?*
  Is this the best time to present the idea, and expect the group members to be in the frame of mind to consider it and share in its development?

- *Am I the person?*
  Am I the best person to present the idea, or would it have a better chance for success if it were presented by someone else?

THE GOAL IS TO STIMULATE ACTION

The experienced conference leader knows that when group members take an active part in the conference proceedings and help shape the decisions reached, they will not only contribute valuable experience and ideas of their own but will also be preconditioned to take action on the decisions because they had a part in making them.

In other words, the leader understands people and what makes people take action. The leader knows that the first step toward action is a realization of need, and that every member of every conference group is, either consciously or unconsciously, asking the question, "What does this mean to me?"

When the answer to this question comes from a member of the group itself, it becomes part of the group's thinking, and prepares the members to take the next steps toward attainment of the conference objective.

HOW DOES THE CONFERENCE LEADER AVOID "BEING STUCK" WITH THE QUESTION?

Let's assume that the conference has as its objective how to make the most effective use of a new company procedure for recruiting clerical staff members. The contents of the recruiting manual have been thoroughly studied and discussed.

The question is asked by one of the newer members of the group, "I think I understand all the procedures we are to follow *after* we have found the recruits, but where is the best place to look for them?"

Many good suggestions on where to look for recruits are contained in the procedure manual—but it is easy to see that this particular phase of the problem is of special concern to this group member.

As conference leader, you may be tempted to refer the questioner to the proper pages in the manual, and move on to the next question. But your objective is not only to achieve understanding, but to *stimulate action*—the right kind of action—when the members return to their jobs.

Rephrase the Question

Instead of yielding to temptation, rephrase the question and "lob" it to the group something like this:

> "Dave has asked a good question. He wants to know more about where to look for the kind of recruits we need. Who has had some experience with this?"

Once the ball has been picked up by a group member, follow through to make sure the member has given the group a clear and complete idea of ways of solving the problem—and that the suggested ways are right.

Two Forks in the Road

If the ideas the group member has expressed are within the company's policy on recruiting, you can simply say thanks and ask for experiences from other group members.

If, on the other hand, you feel that the suggested methods of recruiting are not acceptable, it is important that these mistaken ideas not be allowed to stand uncorrected. Obviously, it would again be easy to correct the error yourself and move on to the next question. But you have a great opportunity at this point, both to check the knowledge of the group and to make sure that everyone present understands and accepts the corporately approved procedure.

Ask questions such as:

> "Elaine has given us her ideas on this. How do these line up with the guidelines in the procedure manual?"

> "Thanks, Elaine. Now let's get another viewpoint on this. Howard, what have you found to be the best sources for the right kind of recruits?"

Answer Only as a Last Resort

If your purpose is to get free participation from members of the group, answer the question yourself only as a last resort. Even then, if possible, address a question to a resource person or to a member of the group you believe has the right answer. There will be some cases where you *must* give the answer, but they are rare.

QUESTION 13

HOW CAN THE LEADER USE QUESTIONS TO GET THE DISCUSSION STARTED, KEEP THE CONFERENCE ON THE TRACK, AND ARRIVE AT AN ACCEPTABLE CONCLUSION?

Questions are your master key not only to get discussion started, keep the conference on the track, and arrive at an acceptable conclusion, but to solve almost any conference problem that may arise.

GETTING THE DISCUSSION STARTED

Usually the best way to get discussion started early in a conference—or to revive discussion as the conference progresses—is to toss out a shotgun question and wait until someone in the group picks it up.

Sometimes, as we said earlier, it seems that the question will never be answered. The silence is deafening and the time gap seems endless. Actually, if you check the time with a stopwatch, you will find that it is usually much less than a minute—and the "strategic wait" is worthwhile.

When you feel you have waited long enough and still do not have a reply, you can simply rephrase the question, throw it back to the group or an individual, and play the waiting game again.

> For example: You have asked the group, "What is the best way to try for a close in a situation like this?"

> It seems to you that you have waited for minutes and you want to prod the group to participate. So you re-phrase the question, and this time direct the question to an individual. You ask, "Bob, you have a good record as a closer, how would you close this one?"

> Or you might ask, "Gail, will you give us an example of a good closing procedure in this situation?"

KEEPING THE DISCUSSION ON THE TRACK

Every conference leader has been up against the situation in which the discussion strays far from the subject. Or perhaps an argument develops that leads the conferees afield. How can the leader bring the group's attention back to the main topic?

A properly phrased question can often do the trick with-out upsetting any of the conferees or making them feel they have been cut off. Simply thank the participants for their ideas up to this point and switch the discussion with a ques-tion like this:

> "Now, with that background, Diane, will you give us your experience on. . . ."

At this point you introduce a new subject which takes you back to your main conference line, and move ahead from there. To sum up, there are two simple steps: first, thank the group for contributions made up to this point; second, "piggyback" a brand-new question that brings you back into position to move ahead.

ARRIVING AT AN ACCEPTABLE CONCLUSION

Obviously, if you are to arrive at an acceptable conclusion, you must develop a conference plan. Otherwise you'll never know what an acceptable conclusion is.

You have used questions to get the discussion started, to keep the discussion going, and to stimulate ideas. You have sounded out every aspect of the problem or project under discussion.

Now the time has come to see whether you have arrived at a consensus in the group. Use consensus-type questions like, "How does the group feel about this?" "Are we pretty well agreed?" "Shall we summarize?"

It is not necessary, nor is it usually advisable, to take a vote or have a head count of pros and cons. Agreement can usually be assumed from the general attitude and response of the group. However, if dissent is expressed, it is important to follow it through. Invite a fuller expression of viewpoint with a question like, "Why do you feel that way about it, Anne?" or "What are your ideas on this, Bob?"

Once the ideas are on the table and fully aired, you can determine whether the group is generally thinking alike or, if there are serious differences, whether you can make adjustments that will lead the group to an acceptable conclusion.

HOW QUESTIONS CAN HELP YOU

Here are some of the many ways that questions can help you from the moment the conference opens until the last objective is reached:

- Get the conference going with participation.
- Keep the group interested by seeing that members continue to take part.
- Guide all the participants toward the conference objective.
- Make sure all get a chance to express themselves.
- Test the group to see if you are really communicating.
- Keep the discussion moving so that one or two group members don't take over.
- Check progress at any time during the conference.
- Get commitments for action from individual members.
- Attain your conference objective—"Make your sale."

Master the use of the question and you will master the art of conference leadership.

QUESTION 14
WHAT IS THE BEST WAY TO SUMMARIZE A CONFERENCE AND MAKE SURE THE DESIRED ACTION WILL BE TAKEN?

As with almost every problem or situation you meet as a conference leader, there is no *one best way* to summarize or make sure you get the action that you set as your conference objective.

Summarizing a conference is much like closing a sale. There is no magic moment when a charmed word is spoken and the customer decides to buy. It is much more likely that some question you asked, some need you uncovered, led the customer to think about satisfying her or his need long before you asked the closing question, "Mrs. Jones, which would you prefer, the yellow or the blue?"

SUMMARIZE AS YOU GO

One of the ablest conference leaders I know stops and gets a "receipt" from his group many times as the conference progresses. One technique he uses is to go around the conference table at key points in the conference and ask each member a question like, "Will you tell us what you have gained from the conference so far?" Then, using the chart pad, he summarizes what they say and gets their agreement that the summary meets their approval. If approval is not complete, he either explains the differences or makes any changes the members request.

Some conference leaders prefer to select one of the group members or have a volunteer come to the chart pad and prepare the summary. After the summary is agreed to, it is posted where it can be seen by everyone in the room.

A Good Time for a Recess

Usually it's a good time for a coffee break when a summary has been made and the direction of the conference may be about to change, or at least to move into new territory.

When a series of summaries has been prepared, and each agreed to by the group, there is really no problem in preparing the final summary. Neither is there any question of whether the members are in agreement.

Plan Your Summaries in Advance

This may sound like "rigging" the conference in order to make sure your predetermined objective is reached, but it is not. When you plan your summaries and subsummaries in advance and you have them *written down* in your notes, you are in a position to check the summaries made by the conferees to see whether any major points have been omitted. When this is the case, a simple question addressed to the group, "What about Jane's point on getting approvals in advance when changes are to be made? Should this be included in the summary?" will make sure you move toward your conference objective.

Summaries Are a Good Way to Get Agreement

When, as so often happens even in the best-planned conference, there seems to be a considerable difference of opinion even after full discussion, a well-planned summary can often smooth the way and restore agreement on major points.

Keep Summaries Participative

Even though the conference itself may have been heavy on presentation, you will usually find it helpful to make the summary as participative as possible. This is just another way to say "use the time-honored technique of playback" to get a reading on how much understanding and acceptance you have been able to achieve. Without participation you can't have feedback.

FOLLOWING THROUGH FOR ACTION

The second part of the question is, "What is the best way to make sure the desired action will be taken?" The answer may well be the measure of the success of your conference. If you have encouraged participation by the members of the group and if you have summarized their reactions, you know without much doubt whether your conference objectives have been achieved. It is a fair conclusion that, given the necessary follow through, the acceptance you have received will be turned into the desired action.

Make an Assignment

One of the most practical ways to measure what has been accomplished in the conference is to give an assignment to be completed and reported on within a given short period of time. If possible have the reports submitted directly to you with copies to the immediate superior involved. Follow through to make sure the assignment is completed and check particularly on any problems or questions that may be involved.

Report Back to the Group

Whether or not a specific assignment is made, summarize the meeting in writing and see that every conferee receives a copy

within a week from the adjournment date. If the conference
is simply a working session lasting an hour or two, or even
less, prepare a report and get it into the hands of the
conferees the next day if possible. Use the summaries and
subsummaries as the basis for the report, adding whatever ex-
planation or elaboration may seem appropriate.

Take advantage of another feedback opportunity and
ask for comments, additions, corrections, or changes of any
kind that the conferees may suggest.

Personal Follow Through

Probably the best way to make sure the desired action is ob-
tained is to check into the situation yourself. If the conferees
are conveniently available check with them personally. If
they have dispersed to other locations call them or arrange a
trip that will take you into their area. In either case don't be
satisfied with secondhand evidence if you can see for yourself.

Hold a Follow-up Meeting

When possible arrange for a follow-up meeting in which each
conferee can report progress and raise any questions or problems he or she may wish to discuss. Often such a meeting can
not only be used to clear the air of problems and give you
firsthand information on the action being taken, but also lead
the way to the next logical step toward achievement of long-
range objectives.

Don't forget the story about the Quaker meeting: "Service begins when the meeting is over."

15

WHAT ARE THE PRINCIPAL BARRIERS TO EFFECTIVE LISTENING BY THE CONFERENCE LEADER AND HOW CAN THEY BE OVERCOME?

Being a good listener is one of the conference leader's essential skills—and one for which he or she is often woefully unprepared. The road to achievement of this essential skill is littered with obstacles, any one of which may lead the conference to failure.

In the context of conference leadership, being a good listener means much more than hearing and understanding words. It means keeping all five senses sharp and in focus, and adding to them a sixth sense which may well be called "the listening spirit," the sincere desire to understand as well as to be understood.

To put all these senses to work and at the same time avoid the pitfalls of personal prejudice, preconceptions, and preconditioning is the highest expression of the leader's art.

WHAT HAPPENS TO A CONFERENCE LEADER?

Suddenly you find yourself standing before a selected conference group, charged with the responsibility of achieving some kind of objective. The most natural conclusion is that the group members look to you for your ideas and opinions on the subject.

The mere fact that you are standing before them is enough to justify that conclusion. To make this conclusion doubly authoritative the group members themselves probably have the same idea.

They may be thinking to themselves, "Well, here we are, conference leader. You gathered us together. I hope you know your stuff and that you give it to us without wasting our time. If you don't have anything important, or at least interesting, to say I'll just turn off my hearing aid and enjoy a well-deserved rest."

The temptations are great to take the offered spotlight to expound on the subject and then, if time permits, to ask, "Are there any questions?" This is especially true if you are the supervisor of the group as well as the conference leader.

Yet if you yield to this double temptation—the temptations of physical position and authority—you cannot listen effectively, and your conference is doomed to failure. If your conferences fail, your personal success as a business or professional leader will be in jeopardy.

William Ellis and Frank Siedel, in a most remarkable book entitled *How to Win a Conference*, make this pointed comment:

> *A man's ability to get his job of engineering done . . . to get his job of accounting done . . . may well depend upon his ability to navigate skillfully through the intricate maze of conferences which moves the great corporate body today. This ability often outweighs the importance of his ability to engineer, sell, produce, finance, execute or transport; because if he has not the ability to handle the all-powerful, omnipresent American conference, he will not get the chance to engineer, sell, finance and produce.* *

---

*William D. Ellis and Frank Siedel, 1955. *How to Win a Conference*. Englewood Cliffs, N.J.: Prentice-Hall, p. 4. Quoted by permission of the publisher.

OBSTACLES TO PERCEPTIVE LISTENING

Listening is a difficult process under the most favorable conditions and—as every conference leader knows all too well—the conditions in a conference situation are rarely completely favorable. It is what the conference leader does, often in the earliest moments, that controls these conditions.

The "Hidden Agenda"

The "hidden agenda" are the individual sets of important matters that occupy conferees' minds as they enter the conference room. They may be worrying about a problem at home or still trying to win an argument that began at lunch yesterday on the Middle East situation. They may be occupied with questions such as, "Will I be able to tee off in time—or will this darned conference last all afternoon?"

The hidden agenda of each conferee are different from anyone else's, and as conference leader you rarely have any idea what is on them. Getting through the smog of all these differing agenda calls for the smartest and most perceptive listening the conference leader can muster.

The Speaking–Listening Gap

It doesn't take deep thought to realize that it is easier to talk than it is to listen. However, most of us don't realize that there is a simple mathematical reason for this.

> The average rate of speech of most Americans is around 125 words a minute whereas we can comprehend speech at the rate of more than 300 words a minute without any significant loss in understanding.

What effect does this have on the ability of the conference leader to listen? Simply this. When a member of the group is speaking, the leader may feel "way ahead of the speaker" and mentally relax or start planning what to say next.

This speed lag between speaking and listening is at the root of much of our listening trouble, both in conferences and face to face.

Stresses and Strains

Under the stresses and strains of conference leadership perceptive listening becomes even more difficult. When the leader is also the group supervisor the pressures of management and of personal and corporate objectives often overpower the leader and the ability to listen perceptively is impaired.

Legend has it that this admonition hangs somewhere in the Pentagon:

> IF YOU CAN KEEP YOUR HEAD WHILE
> ALL ABOUT YOU ARE LOSING THEIRS—
> YOU DON'T UNDERSTAND THE SITUATION.

Many a conference leader has lost the power to listen simply by becoming personally involved in the problem being discussed and being carried away with preconceived biases or opinions. The leader may feel completely in control even when "emotional filters" have overpowered the ability to listen perceptively. As a result, listening is overcome by the desire to talk. Conference leadership suffers.

"Tunnel Listening"

The temptation to become wrapped up in your own objectives often leads to a malady known as "tunnel listening." Your mind is so completely centered on your own line of thought or your own preconceived destination that you cannot clearly hear sounds or any other evidences which point in another direction.

The term "tunnel listening" is patterned after the more familiar expression "tunnel vision," a defect that usually results from being overtired or under the influence of a depressant such as alcohol. The individual tries too hard to focus on an immediate objective and therefore loses all consciousness of what is happening at the sides. Peripheral vision is cut off. Tunnel listening is much the same. Although it can be good to the extent that it targets your listening entirely on the immediate goal, it can be bad because it reduces your sensitivity to group reactions. Thus it is a threat to perceptive listening.

"Corporate Blinders"

Close kin to tunnel listening is the condition in which the conference leader is equipped with "corporate blinders"— the tendency to shut out anything from consciousness that is not in accord with the corporate line. If the conference leader is aware of a countercorporate comment made by a group member, he or she immediately kicks it from consciousness by labeling it "contrary to our policy."

"Hardening of the Categories"

Another close relative of corporate blinders and tunnel listening is the progressive problem of "hardening of the categories"—a deadly threat to effective listening. Hardening of the categories sets in when we think we have found all the answers and filed them away in airtight compartments to be held changeless for all time. Everyone is susceptible to this creeping paralysis, but with a conference leader it is a deadly affliction.

"Emotional Filters"

Every conference leader is subject to the destructive effects of "emotional filters." Dr. Nichols in *Are You Listening?* describes what happens when the emotional filters are at work:

> *In different degrees and in many different ways, listening ability is affected by our emotions. Figuratively we reach up and mentally turn off what we do not want to hear. Or, on the other hand, when someone says what we especially want to hear, we open our ears wide, accepting everything—truths, half-truths, or fiction. We might say, then, that our emotions act as aural filters. At times they in effect cause deafness, and at other times they make listening altogether too easy.* *

---

* Ralph G. Nichols and Leonard A. Stevens, 1957. *Are You Listening?* New York: McGraw-Hill, p. 90. Quoted by permission of the publisher.

Prejudging, Ambiguity, and Illusion

When a conference leader yields to the temptation to prejudge the comments made by any member of the group his or her ability to listen perceptively reaches an all-time low. Often, because of the density of the filter, the leader doesn't even know he or she is prejudging. When this kind of emotional involvement exists, reason flies out the window and communication breaks down.

Ambiguity is a threat to perceptive listening only when it creeps in without being announced and is not recognized. The conference leader is sure that he or she has understood correctly and the group member feels equally sure his or her statement is crystal clear. This combination of circumstances is the most insidious of all the obstacles that face the conference leader in the effort to listen perceptively.

William H. Whyte, Jr., in his book *Is Anybody Listening?* makes this comment:

> *The great enemy of communication is the illusion of it. We have talked enough; but we have not listened. And by not listening, we have failed to concede the immense complexity of our society* [or our conference group]— *and thus the great gaps between ourselves and those with whom we seek understanding.* *

These are only a few of the many obstacles you face in your quest for perceptive listening and group understanding. Each obstacle has its own endless variations and combinations that present a constantly changing spectrum of dilemmas each with its own individual solution.

MORE HINTS ON EFFECTIVE LISTENING

Listen for Understanding

Before you make up your mind on what a group member means, make sure you understand not only the facts being ex-

---

*William H. Whyte, Jr., 1952. *Is Anybody Listening?* New York: Simon and Schuster, p. 38. Quoted by permission of the publisher.

pressed but also the speaker's ideas and feelings about those facts. To do this keep all your senses tuned in and sensitive to the situation so that you know *when* and *how* to ask the key questions, and *to whom* to direct them.

As with nearly every other conference situation, the right question asked in the right way and at the right time is the key to perceptive listening—and to successful conference leadership.

Listen to the Silence

Listen to the silence as well as to the words. Silence is one of the most eloquent communicators of all.

Prolonged silence may indicate approval, disapproval, embarrassment, uncertainty, or a period of mental gestation. Facial expressions, movements of the body, or shuffling feet may help you understand the real meaning of the silence.

Beware of Involvement

The real test of a conference leader as a professional is the ability to preserve a "psychical distance" from the group members and at the same time to be completely sensitive to the ideas and feelings of the group.

This does not mean lack of interest or lack of leadership. Perhaps it is best compared to the difference between "empathy" and "sympathy." Sympathy is suffering along with another. Empathy is understanding the other's problems but still not becoming personally involved.

No part of your work as a conference leader is more difficult than avoiding personal involvement. Yet it is a prerequisite of perceptive listening.

Guard against Prejudging, Ambiguity, and Illusion

To combat the tendency to prejudge, the successful conference leader assumes a professional attitude and does not become personally embroiled in the other person's problem but instead hears the speaker out and does not discount in advance what the speaker has to say.

To dispel ambiguity the conference leader asks the participant to explain his or her views more fully and to give examples of what he or she has in mind. "Tell us more" is often a good expression to combat ambiguity and ensure understanding.

To make sure that understanding is not an illusion, the leader carefully weighs the evidence supplied by all the senses, and by repeated use of questions determines whether true communication has been achieved.

THE "LISTENING SPIRIT"

When you follow these guideposts in the "listening spirit"— with the sincere desire to understand what your conference group is telling you—you will be well on your way to overcoming the most persistent barriers to effective listening. And you will have followed the golden rule of listening, "Listen to others as you would have them listen to you."

HOW CAN THE CONFERENCE LEADER AVOID THE TEMPTATION TO JUMP TO CONCLUSIONS ABOUT WHAT IS HEARD FROM THE CONFEREES?

Many years ago in New York I had a boss who had a sign on his desk with these words in giant black type:

NEVER ASSUME ANYTHING.

I'm not sure that life—or conferences—would be possible without making some assumptions but it pays to be aware of the dangers we run in conference leadership when assumptions are not justified.

If you practice the golden rule of listening, you won't have to worry about the temptation to jump to conclusions. Like other human beings, however, conference leaders sometimes run out of patience or feel the pressure of time before they have heard the other person out. As a result they may make unwarranted assumptions.

HEAR THEM OUT

The best protection against making false or premature conclusions is to hear the other person out. Try to listen from *the other's* point of view rather than your own. This often means you must fight your emotional filters that keep telling you how wrong he or she is. The more they tell you this, the more difficult it is to listen from the other's point of view.

There are occasions, of course, when because of shortness of time or other pressures it is necessary to shut off a conferee, but these occasions are rare. When you do this you run the risk of destroying the permissive climate you have worked hard to establish, and of discouraging, if not completely cutting off, further group participation.

> I recall vividly a conference situation in which all the salespeople and sales managers of a large company had been called together to learn the details of a sensational new product that the company was about to announce with a $ million advertising campaign.
>
> The sales vice-president, who was chairperson of the meeting, called for questions from the floor. After the usual period of embarrassed silence, or "pregnant pause" as Dr. Dee calls it, a sales agent stood up and asked a question which the chairperson felt was completely out of order.
>
> Instead of probing deeper to find out what the person was really trying to ask, or to use this as an opportunity to dispel any similar disturbing questions, the vice-president slapped the person down in front of 300 or so of the person's co-workers as well as the person's immediate boss. Obviously this was the end of questions from the floor.

When you encourage the conferees to express themselves, you not only benefit from better understanding of what they think and how they feel but you also protect the permissive nature of the conference. You automatically encourage others to express their opinions without fear of being squelched or ruled out of order.

PRESS FOR MORE INFORMATION

Don't be satisfied with the ideas expressed by conferees unless and until you are clear about what they mean *from their*

frame of reference. Make sure that the point has been made completely, and that there is no "irritating remainder."

One of the most effective conference leaders I have ever seen was at his best when he ran into "flak" from members of a group who seemed unable to understand or unwilling to accept the point of view of the conference as a whole.

Like a clutch player with two outs and the bases loaded, he remained as calm as ever in this kind of tense situation. Instead of "losing his cool" and taking the dissidents apart, which his rank would have permitted, he used every tool in the conference leader's kit to achieve understanding.

He probed in depth with questions like, "Just what part of the program do you feel should be changed?" or, "What do you think management should do about this?" or simply, "Tell us more about your ideas on this."

As a consequence the misunderstandings that had caused the dissension generally melted away and, with the support of the rest of the group, the conference moved to its predetermined objective. Not a feather was ruffled and no one had been put on the spot.

BUT TIME MUST MARCH ON

Obviously it is not always possible to probe in depth into every viewpoint and into every idea expressed in the conference, because time is usually limited—it marches on.

One of the best ways to bring a lengthy comment to a close and make sure you understand fully the thoughts and feelings of the conferee making the comment is to rephrase the idea as clearly as you know how and ask the conferee whether this states the idea to his or her satisfaction. If you get agreement, you can be sure that you understand each other. Then you can try the rephrased comment on the rest of the group, ask their reactions and questions, and make sure everyone understands the point.

This takes time, and the amount of discussion must be controlled accordingly. If your purpose is to conclude this phase of the discussion and move on to another subject, one way to do it is to thank the conferees making the point and direct a rifle question to another conferee like this:

"Lynn, you have had experience with another important phase of this problem. What have you found is the best way to evaluate results?"

THE HEART OF THE PROBLEM

The problem of how to avoid making unwarranted assumptions is like many others you will face in conference work in that at the heart of the problem is the basic need to cultivate the listening spirit—the sincere desire to understand *with* the other person. It takes patience, self-restraint, and much practice to acquire and apply this spirit but it is the benchmark of excellence. It is your best protection against the temptation to jump to conclusions.

QUESTION 17

HOW CAN THE CONFERENCE LEADER MAKE SURE HE OR SHE UNDERSTANDS NOT ONLY WHAT THE CONFEREES *SAY* BUT ALSO WHAT THEY REALLY MEAN?

Seeing into another person's mind is difficult, and understanding what you see is even more of an achievement. Yet seeing into the minds of assorted members of a conference group and understanding what they think and how they feel may be easier than you think. As was pointed out earlier, the conference leader has a tool designed to help open the minds of conferees and see what is going on inside.

THE MIND OPENER

Questions, properly framed, directed, and followed up, are the mind openers, the mental Geiger counters that can spot with uncanny accuracy what the conferees are thinking. But, however revealing the question, the true meaning of the response can be revealed only by listening perceptively. If questions are the mind *openers*, then perceptive listening is the mind *reader*.

95

LISTEN TO THE IDEAS

Listen to the ideas your conferees express in reply to your question. How do they express them? Are their words cool and logical, indicating that the conferees are seriously trying to solve the problem and make a genuine contribution? Are they loaded with emotion or do they express prejudice and antagonism? If the words are loaded with emotional freight, the real idea that is coming through may have little, if any, relationship to what the conferee is saying.

LISTEN TO THE FEELINGS BEHIND THE WORDS

Be sensitive to *how* the words are said as well as *what* they say. When the speaker's voice is raised in excitement, you are getting a message that there is unexpressed pressure behind the comment. One way to treat this situation is to open the communicational pipelines and let the pressure come through. This can be done by inviting the conferee to "tell us more" or "give us the whole story." Once the story is out in the open, the pressure will be relieved and you will find what the conferee really means.

LISTEN FOR THE SILENCE

Often the most revealing action is for a conferee to suddenly "clam up." You don't know what to think. What does this mean? Does this mean agreement? Disagreement? Does it simply show lack of interest? It could mean any of these or it might be that the conferee is just thinking it over and trying to arrive at a meaningful answer.

Silence is a medium of communication in just as true a sense as spoken words are but silence is much more difficult to interpret. Obviously, the first step is to break the silence.

Often you can do this just by waiting the conferee out. The sheer pressure of silence may lead the person to express the idea he or she has in mind. Discreet, well-planned questioning may help to break the ice and get the flow of communication opened again. Too much questioning may simply drive the conferee's ideas further underground. If your efforts aren't successful, move on to another subject and come back to this one at a more appropriate time.

GROUP INTERACTION—A TRUTH SERUM

As has been said earlier, groups do not have feelings. Only individuals do. However, group interaction influences feelings in curious ways, many of which are not fully understood.

At the opening of a conference the individuals may have a tendency to avoid participating because they are afraid they may expose some area of ignorance to the leader and their peers. As the session progresses, the members are likely to be more venturesome and outspoken than they would be if questioned individually face to face.

The power of free discussion among conferees often releases ideas that no amount of individual probing would uncover. One idea leads to another. One experience suggests another. One statement leads to confirmation or denial by other members of the group. Use this power of group interaction to make sure that the words being spoken express the actual feelings of your conferees.

WHAT HAPPENS WHEN THE BOSS IS PRESENT?

Often when the boss is present there is a tendency on the part of the group to withhold their comments or to tailor them to what they think the boss wants to hear. In some cases, as conference leader you are also the boss. When you are, you are faced with a doubly difficult assignment.

> I recall an incident in which, with the general manager's consent—in fact with his urging—all his district sales managers were called together for a conference under the guidance of a trusted, but disinterested, staff member.
>
> The meeting was opened wide with the statement, "As everyone in this room knows, our sales have been below quota for the last several months. We want you to help us find out what the trouble is."

Response was slow in coming but when it did come it was a bombshell. "The trouble is the general manager. Until he learns how to delegate responsibility to the DSM's, we're not going to get anywhere."

When told about this later the general manager was big enough to see the truth in the criticism and the problem was corrected. But it would have been impossible had the manager been present.

As a general rule, when the real ideas and feelings of the group are to be clearly expressed and understood, it's better if the direct line boss is busy elsewhere. As with all rules, however, you will find many exceptions.

THE POWER OF PARTICIPATION

When you have established a truly permissive atmosphere, and when you have won the confidence of the group that their ideas are not only welcome but necessary to the success of the conference, you will have gone a long way toward not only seeing into the minds of your conferees but reading their feelings as well.

QUESTION **18**

HOW CAN AN
UNDERSTANDING OF SEMANTICS
HELP THE CONFERENCE LEADER?

When you understand and accept the fact that words have different meanings to different people, you have a running start toward effective communication with your conferees.

MEANINGS ARE IN PEOPLE

David Berlo, in his book *The Process of Communication*,* makes the point that meanings are not in words but in people. Every person, through individual experiences, attaches different shades of meaning to words. Sometimes these differences are slight and have little effect on communication. Sometimes they are great and may become insurmountable barriers.

---

*David K. Berlo, 1960. *The Process of Communication*. New York: Holt, Rinehart and Winston, p. 174.

Take, for example, the statement, "I think that John is at heart a communist." In some business and political circles this statement could lead to dismissal or ostracism or both. In Moscow the statement would be high praise and might well lead to an advancement in the party and in society.

Like many other words, the word "semantics" means many things to many people and nothing at all to others. A fairly good working definition of semantics as a basis for conference work is "what words mean to people." In a conference there may be as many shades of meaning to a given word as there are people in the conference.

Meaning Is in the Listener

What a word means to each listener is just as important as what the word means to the leader. If you mean one thing when you use the word, and one or more of your conferees interpret it differently, the result will be a breakdown in communication. As we discussed earlier, the breakdown can be most deadly when both you and your conferees think you understand each other. You have the *illusion* of communication.

As an example of how many different meanings can be conveyed by a single word, consider the common word "file."

- To a private secretary or a clerk "file" may mean a steel file drawer.
- To the boss or secretary "file" may bring to mind the folder in which customer information is stored.
- To a carpenter a "file" is an instrument for smoothing a piece of wood.
- To a convict it might mean a rat-tail file to cut through a steel bar.
- To a soldier it may suggest "standing in single file."

Meanings are in people and it is their individual experiences and present interests that govern the message they receive from the word.

WORDS MAKE SENTENCES

What applies to words applies as well to phrases and sentences. Even one word, when improperly communicated, can alter the meaning of an entire sentence or a complete proposal.

At a meeting in Geneva between U.S. and Soviet representatives the United States delegate opened the session by suggesting that a certain subject be "tabled."

The result of the suggestion was immediate objection by the Russian spokesman, who then gathered his delegates and stormed out of the meeting.

The reason, it was discovered later, is that to the Russians the term "tabled" meant "to bring to the table for discussion." To the Americans, it meant just the opposite—"to put aside and take up the rest of the agenda."

A semantic difference, in this case, turned what might have been agreement into a disagreement so violent that it broke up the meeting.

SEMANTIC GUIDEPOSTS

In *The Power of Words* Stuart Chase interprets the semantic guideposts of Alfred Korzybski, the founder of General Semantics, in a way that can help any conference leader communicate more effectively with his conferees. For Chase's full interpretation turn to Chapter 13 of the book. Reading it will be well worthwhile.

Following is a brief comment on each of Korzybski's five guideposts, presented with the conference leader especially in mind:

"Quotes"

Use abstract words and phrases like "the American Way" or "leftist" or "extremist" only with the understanding that they must be defined unless everyone present has the same concept of them. The same is true of unusual words like "rubric" or technical words like "programming" or "COBOL."

As conference leader you have the responsibility of making sure that you and the conferees attach the same meanings to the words you use.

"Indexes"

Qualify as exactly as you can what kind of object, situation, or idea you are referring to. For example, the word "apple" is simple enough, but just what kind of apple do you have in mind: a Russet?—or a Delicious? Be specific and, if possible, use pictures to avoid misunderstanding. Korzybski qualifies with index numbers: $Apple^1$, $Apple^2$, etc.

"Dates"

Specify the exact date and time of any reference. For example, England (1588) in the time of Elizabeth I, differs from England (1776), and again from England (1979).

The exact phase of the moon was the key point that swayed the jury to render a verdict of "not guilty" in one of Abraham Lincoln's famous trials.

In a conference the dates and times you establish can avoid confusion and help you reach your predetermined objective.

"Hyphens"

Words must be put together in series to create clear mental images. As we showed with the word "file," single words mean little standing by themselves. It's the way they are used, and the words around them, that determine their meaning. Again, pictures and diagrams will go a long way toward giving meaning to the words.

"Etc."

Probably the most important guidepost of all to the conference leader is the little abbreviation "etc." As we all know, this abbreviation stands for the words "et cetera" and it simply means, "That's really not all there is to it but it's all the detail we have time for here."

The word "etc." expresses the idea that however completely you try to paint a picture with a word, a phrase or a sentence, there is always much more that has not been covered.

Recognizing this incompleteness, the conference leader should mentally add "etc." to any thought expressed, and realize that the same incompleteness applies to the statements made by the conferees, etc.

UNDERSTANDING BOTH WAYS

One of your prime objectives as conference leader is to make sure you understand your conferees and they understand you. Knowing the meaning of the word "semantics" and following its guidelines can help you in presenting your ideas, in questioning, and in effective listening to make sure that understanding goes both ways.

QUESTION **19**

HOW CAN THE CONFERENCE LEADER TELL HOW LONG TO KEEP PARTICIPATION GOING AND WHEN TO CLOSE IT OFF?

Too much participation can wear the conferees' interest thin and they may go away feeling that they have gained little from the time spent. Not enough participation can effectively turn off attention and lead to a dull conference. As conference leader you strive for the perfect blend of participation and presentation—the blend that gives the group the knowledge they need and gives you a clear indication that you have achieved your objective.

The best mix of participation and presentation may never be the same from one conference to another but here are some guidelines drawn from the experience of many conference leaders.

HAVE A WRITTEN CONFERENCE PLAN

Probably your most useful guide is a carefully prepared, written conference plan that contains all the major points you expect to make—whether through presentation or participation.

A quick check of the plan at any point in the conference will tell you how far you have gone and how much more ground you still have to cover. It will give you an instant clue as to whether you should dig deeper for more ideas from the group or whether it's time to summarize and lead to adjournment.

THE CONFERENCE CLOCK

Nearly every conference has some time limit. Usually there is a set time for the session to be concluded and it's up to you to finish on time. An occasional look at the clock will prepare you for the time when you should close off participation. If you find that it will not be possible to cover all the ground you had planned, you may decide to set a new date for a follow-up conference. If this is not possible the clock will tell you when to cut off group comments entirely and cover the final points by direct presentation.

DON'T RUSH THE GROUP

How many times have you heard a conference leader say something like, "We only have a few minutes left, so let's have two more quick questions." The feeling of being pressed for time gets to the group instantly and participation stops.

If your purpose is to wind up the conference, summarize the progress made, cover any final points, and adjourn the meeting. The last-minute call for "quick questions" is usually an exercise in futility.

TAKE THE TEMPERATURE OF THE GROUP

The temperature or interest of your conferees often tells you when a discussion should be terminated and another subject introduced. Questions like, "Do you feel that this discussion is helpful?" or "Would you like to dig deeper into this subject?" will help you take the group's temperature. The interest they express will help you decide whether to continue the discussion or move ahead with the next point.

LEAD TO A PROPER CONCLUSION

As discussed earlier, it is your responsibility as conference leader to guide the group to a proper conclusion. You can't duck this responsibility. If you find that it is not possible to conclude the subject in this session, plan another session or arrange to provide the missing information in some other way.

Most conference leaders agree that it is bad practice to break off an incomplete discussion with a comment like, "Well, it's too bad, but we don't have time to complete this subject, so let's move ahead to the next point." The result of this kind of comment is frustration and a feeling of bewilderment on the part of the group.

Instead, complete each section of the conference satisfactorily even if this means that participation must be cut back. As we all know, the pressure of time sometimes makes it difficult to get the ideas of all the conferees, but with proper planning and effective control you can usually achieve your conference objectives in the time available.

How long should you keep participation going? Probably the best answer is to keep it going as long as you feel the results are worthwhile, as long as the conferees are interested, and the clock and the conference plan permit.

QUESTION 20
WHAT TYPES OF AUDIOVISUAL AIDS ARE MOST USEFUL IN CONFERENCE LEADERSHIP?

As with so many other questions on conference leadership, there is no pat answer to this one. The type or types of media that will be most helpful depend on a number of conditions: the purpose of the meeting, the nature and size of the group, the location and facilities available, and the personal preferences and skills of the leader.

The presentation tools you use should be selected after studying all the conditions involved, including cost and the time and talent available for preparation and presentation.

PREPARATION OF VISUALS

In preparing visuals, or in selecting them from available materials, keep in mind that their primary purpose is to deliver a quick, clear message, not to be decorative, tricky, or artistic. They should be easy to read and understand. They do *not* need to be beautiful.

Size of type or lettering, amount of white space, simplicity of illustration, and neatness and clarity are of major importance. Homemade visuals are fine when they fit the subject and deliver the message effectively. Professionally prepared visuals, properly designed and executed, can contribute much to the success of the conference. However good the visuals, in the final analysis the way they are used is the real test.

As this book is concerned primarily with the smaller, more informal types of conferences, visual aids most useful with groups of from 12 to 25 people will be discussed.

HAND TOOLS AND MECHANICAL TOOLS

As conference leader you have two general types of audio-visual aids to choose from—hand tools, which you handle and control personally, and mechanical tools, which are prepared in advance to be projected or played in prearranged sequence.

Examples of hand tools are the chart pad and crayon, the chalkboard, prepared charts of various types, opaque and overhead projection, $2'' \times 2''$ slides, and simple tape recordings. Examples of mechanical tools are sound slidefilms, motion pictures, audio- and videotape, and closed-circuit television.

The line between hand tools and mechanical tools is an indefinite one because some media, such as overhead projection, $2'' \times 2''$ slides, and recordings, require some degree of mechanization. They have been classified arbitrarily as hand tools because their control is entirely in the hands of the meeting leader. They are the leader's tools to be used in the most effective order to illustrate and reinforce points or to provide a means for directing audience participation.

Mechanical tools, on the other hand, once set up for use and turned on, must be shown or played in the order, and generally for the length of time, that the producer intended. With a mechanical medium such as videotape the conference leader and planner may, of course, also be the producer.

Both types of audiovisual aids are useful in conference work and can be effectively used in combination with each other. Both have their advantages and disadvantages. Both require advance preparation and expertise from the conference leader.

Hand Tools

Chart pad. Probably the most useful and versatile tool you as conference leader have is the plain white paper sheet on a chart pad. On it you can record in telegraphic form the ideas the conferees generate. Using each idea as a starting point you can encourage the group to "piggyback" and suggest other ideas until, under your guidance, the subject is fully developed.

You can use the chart pad to provide an outline for discussion and as a means to summarize what has been covered. You can use it to review all the ideas that have been developed, by hanging the individual pages around the walls of the room where they can be seen by the group. You can use it as a basis for preparing a written report for later consideration by yourself, your conferees, and your management. Yet with its usefulness and simplicity, expert use of the chart pad is a rare skill.

Chalkboards. Like the chart pad, the chalkboard provides flexibility. It enables you to generate *with your group* the ideas needed to work toward your conference objective. Obviously the prime drawback of the chalkboard is that it must be erased and, when this happens, all record of the ideas developed is destroyed. Anyone who has used a chalkboard, and that includes most of us, is aware of the problems of chalk dust and the foggy appearance of the board after erasure.

Prepared charts. Where the message is too complex or would be too time-consuming to generate on the chart pad, prepared charts are useful for highlighting your main points or providing a brief outline. The advantages of using color and illustrating key ideas make prepared charts especially effective.

Complicated problems, product comparisons, bar charts, and graphs can be effectively presented on prepared charts when the conference group is not too large.

If you want to reveal a chart progressively, rather than all at once, you can cover a portion of it with a patch of white paper attached with masking tape, or provide a separate piece of white chart board to cover the area to be concealed. This can easily be removed when you're ready to reveal the text.

Flannelboard symbols. The flannelboard has special advantages to the conference leader. Being able to start with a single piece and build a cumulative story is of considerable value. One of the most effective uses of flannelboard is to build a general outline of the subject or subjects to be covered. Each symbol can list or illustrate one of the key points. In this way a series of six or eight points can be established which can then be discussed or presented in more depth by other media such as overhead slides, tape recordings, or printed materials. The completed flannelboard outline can also be used effectively as a summary of the discussion.

As with the chart pad, effective use of flannelboard requires skill and experience in presentation techniques.

Opaque projection. The opaque projector fills a need when there is not enough time or budget to prepare slides. When a subject, such as a new form or procedure, is to be presented only once with a single group, the opaque projector may be the most practical answer to the problem. Awkwardness of projection and the need for a nearly dark room are some of the problems with this medium.

Overhead projection. The overhead projector is ideal for use when you want to project slides on the screen and yet have the benefit of eye contact with the conferees. The brilliance of the image makes it unnecessary to darken the room. Also, this type of projection permits the use of special effects, such as progressive disclosure and transparent overlays, which heighten group interest and make it possible for you to emphasize any part of the picture.

With overhead projection you never have to turn your back on the group to point out features on the screen. You do this on the transparency itself by simply pointing to the area involved or by underlining, checking, or circling a feature on the transparency; this action is shown on the screen as you perform it.

The combination of chart pad, flannelboard, and overhead projection gives a conference a change of pace that enhances the presentation, helps develop participation, and maintains group interest.

$2'' \times 2''$ slides and filmstrips. There are many times in conference work where $2'' \times 2''$ slides provide the most effective visualization. This is especially true when you have a series of pictures to show and you may want to change the order of showing. In general, a $2'' \times 2''$ slide projector requires a darkened room for full screen brilliance. When it is not necessary to change the order of the pictures they may be reproduced on a filmstrip, which takes up much less space and costs substantially less to reproduce in quantity.

Tape recordings. The ease of making tape recordings today makes this audio tool one of increasing interest to conference leaders. Tapes can be made before the conference or during the conference. They have so many varying uses that they cannot be described here. One of the most effective uses is to present a case or situation as the basis for discussion and analysis by the group.

Mechanical Tools

Sound slidefilms. The combination of a strip of still pictures with sound, either on a record or on tape, has proved to be effective in conference use. A wide variety of existing films is available, especially in the sales field.

Although the sound slidefilm does not show motion, dramatic effects can be achieved through quick frame changes, lively music, and dramatic use of voice and sound effects.

One of the most interesting applications of slidefilm is the segmented "stop-and-go" film. The film is prepared in sections, each section dealing with one aspect of the subject. At the end of a segment the room lights are turned on and the group discusses the subject. Then the lights are turned off again and the next segment is shown and its subject matter is discussed as before.

Motion pictures. A sound motion picture in color is the closest thing to real experience that can be used by a conference leader. In some ways—because of camera techniques, close-ups, dissolves, etc.—the motion picture can provide more effective detail of products, people, and their actions than can be seen in real life.

Yet with all its communicative power, effective use of the motion picture depends largely on the ability of the conference leader to introduce it in such a way that it relates to the business of the conference. Unless the picture is concerned directly with the problems of the conferees, the leader must provide a realistic "bridge" so that the conferees see specifically how the film relates to them and the situation being discussed.

Once the bridge has been built, and the film shown, the way the conference leader draws out the views of the conferees makes the difference between "just another entertaining show" and a purposeful audiovisual tool.

Segmented motion pictures. For conference use, the segmented motion picture can be of special interest. The film is written and produced in segments, with each segment covering a specific point or phase of the problem. After each segment are a few feet of opaque film so that the leader can easily see where the segment ends so that he or she can stop the projector for discussion.

As with sound slidefilms, segmenting makes the film of great value to the conference leader in stimulating, guiding, and controlling group discussion.

Videotaped productions. When videotaped programs are produced in advance of a conference, they can be used much like motion pictures. They offer the extra benefit of having been produced specifically for the conference and of relating directly to the problems with which the conferees are confronted. When used live, with closed-circuit television, they add the element of personalization and simultaneous communication.

Computer-assisted training. With more and more institutions in business, government, and education having access to the services of electronic data processing equipment, the conference leader has, in increasing degree, the largely untapped services of this equipment to assist in conference planning. One immediate possibility is in the field of business games and problems. With this amazing new dimension of communication ready to be put to work, instant answers can be provided for even the most complex situation. The uses of EDP in conference planning and conducting have still to be fully explored.

MIXING MEDIA

In most conferences you will be using more than one medium. You may use a motion picture to set up the conditions of a problem, a flannelboard and a chart pad to analyze its cause, and a series of presentation charts or slides to work out the optimum solution.

You may find it effective to use a number of different, but complementary, media within a single segment of the conference. For example, you might introduce the subject using the flannelboard. Then you might use overhead projection to bring out details of the subject. If during the discussion a number of interesting subordinate points are suggested, you might record these on the chart pad or chalkboard. Then, when discussion is completed, you might use flannelboard or chart pad again to wrap up the main points and summarize.

Media should be chosen not simply for change of pace but for the different approaches they bring to the subject and for the effect of their "mix" in helping to achieve your conference objective. The *Check-Chart of Audiovisual Media*, which is reproduced in Table 20.1, may help you select the best media mix to fit your conference plan.

SUPPLEMENTS, NOT SUBSTITUTES

Audiovisual aids are supplements to effective conference leadership—not substitutes for it. Thus the skill of the conference leader and the thorough understanding of how to make the most effective use of presentation tools are more significant than the technical excellence of the audiovisuals the leader uses.

The individual behind the medium makes the real difference. The simplest medium, like a chart pad or chalkboard, can come to life in the hands of a skilled conference leader. On the other hand, the most expensive color motion picture with stereophonic sound may, when ineptly used, make little contribution to the achievement of the conference objective.

Table 20.1 CHECK-CHART OF AUDIOVISUAL MEDIA

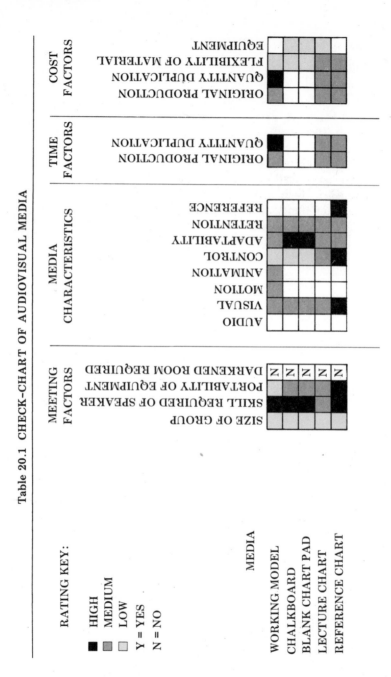

RATING KEY:

■ HIGH
▨ MEDIUM
▢ LOW
Y = YES
N = NO

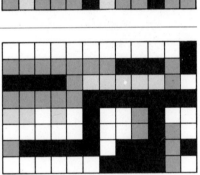

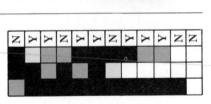

N	FLANNELBOARD
Y	OPAQUE PROJECTION
Y	GLASS SLIDE
N	OVERHEAD PROJECTION
Y	SILENT SLIDEFILM
Y	SILENT MOTION PICTURE
N	ELECTRICAL TRANSCRIPTION
Y	SOUND SLIDEFILM
Y	MOTION SLIDEFILM
Y	SOUND MOTION PICTURE
N	PLAYLET
N	ILLUSTRATED LITERATURE

21

QUESTION
HOW CAN YOU CREATE
GROUP INVOLVEMENT
THROUGH THE USE
OF GAMES, CASES,
AND SIMULATIONS?

Recently I had the opportunity to participate in a game called "Performulations."* The name of the game is a blend of the words performance and simulations. The group of 12 participants was made up of training professionals in the Detroit area. I was teamed with a consulting psychologist, a member of a nationally known firm of management psychologists. I found myself in the interesting position, during the first exercise, of being the psychologist's boss. Next time round, I was his worker.

Along with the other five "bosses," I was called into the next room by the meeting leader and handed a little blue card that read:

> Build a four-sided object
> with something
> hanging in the middle.

---

*TM Creative Universal, Inc., 21700 Northwestern Highway, Southfield, Michigan 48075

No other instructions! So we went back, mystified, to our respective workers where we had been provided with a set of *Tinkertoys*®. The idea, of course, was to use our managerial skills in the best way we could to get our workers to carry out the instructions within the four minutes allotted. Realizing that my worker was not only a psychologist but also a professional meeting leader, I decided that any instructions beyond those on the little blue card would be superfluous. Each of the teams did its best. Our rectangle was complete (with something hanging in the middle!) when the leader called time.

There are many lessons that can be drawn from this exercise, but as "the boss" in this case, I put to work the theory that if your worker knows as much as you do or more about the assigned task, take full advantage of his or her expertise. At least, why get in the way?

THE "PERFORMULATIONS" FORMULA

Harry Lebovitz, general manager of the Products Division of Creative Universal, Inc. describes the "Performulations" formula this way:

> Performulations uses a nonthreatening simulation technique. Participants are paired in teams of boss and worker. In each exercise, the objective is for the bosses to get their workers to build a particular model using TINKERTOY® construction pieces.
>
> Bosses interact with their workers in two ways:
>
> (1) They provide their workers with information about the model to be built.
>
> (2) They react to their workers as they attempt to build the desired model.
>
> Depending on the way the information is provided, and on the way the bosses treat their workers as they attempt to build the model, different results are achieved. The workshop is designed to permit the trainer/instructor to relate the results of each exercise to the on-job experiences of the participants.

The Workshop Format

A typical "Performulations" session follows this sequence of events:

- *Show sound/slide presentation* that introduces the participants to the concepts to be covered.
- *Pair participants into two-person teams* who will play the roles of boss and worker.
- *Conduct the exercise.* In each exercise construction sets are used to build a specific model. This model represents a terminal objective. The "bosses" use various techniques to get their "workers" to accomplish the objective.
- *Discuss the results* of each exercise. Participants relate the results to actual on-the-job situations.
- *The Learner Workbook* provides a worksheet for each of the six exercises to help learners evaluate their newly learned management skills.
- *Conclude with the case studies* in the Learner Workbook to bring together all the experiences in the "Performulations" exercises.
- *An Instructor's Guide* gives complete instructions on how to plan for, conduct, and follow up the session or sessions.

Interest was high in the session I attended. I found myself just as much involved when I was the "worker" as when I was "the boss." Reports from many other users give similar results.

THE "MOTOROLA" GAME

With the keen management interest in subjects related to Equal Employment Opportunity and Affirmative Action, the Motorola game, "EEO—It's Your Job," is a good example of a game designed to teach a specific area of knowledge.

In a dramatic way, the Motorola game applies EEO regulations and concepts and shows the consequences when these regulations are misapplied or disregarded. The game is played like "Monopoly" with four players to a board. The training package contains the following elements:

- A slide presentation explaining the principal regulations of EEO and Affirmative Action.
- A leader's guide including a script to accompany the slide presentation.
- The game board portraying progress through the calendar year and the various potential steps in the discrimination charge procedures.
- 60 case cards offering the players a number of problems and action options.
- Four game markers (one white and one brown male, and one yellow and one black female).
- One die.
- $4 million in play money—$1 million for each player.

How the Game Is Played

After a brief introduction by the leader, the players are assigned to their boards. Play ensues for an hour or so to dramatize the high cost of discrimination and the setbacks that result from poor affirmative action or bad business decisions. The game process emphasizes that EEO is part of everyone's job. Then the series of slides is shown and discussed to cover the law and its application to the specific work environment.

The game is then resumed, reinforcing the learning process and giving the participants an opportunity to apply theory in the solution of practical cases. Discussion follows and the slides may be repeated to clear up any points of law or procedure.

The game is designed for all levels of management, particularly first line and middle management. It can be purchased from Motorola, Inc., 1303 Algonquin Road, Schaumburg, Illinois 60196.

The Game Objective

The objective is to answer the questions presented on the case cards correctly so that players move around the board quickly and conserve their cash. The case cards depict experiences similar to those faced daily by the manager. They cover the entire range of discrimination situations including race, sex, age, religion, handicap, and national origin.

The gameboard represents an entire calendar compliance year and is divided into quarters.

Each player starts off with a budget of $1 million and a game marker. Play begins when the person closest to January 1 draws a case card from the deck on the gameboard. The player reads aloud the first case card and chooses one of several answers to the case in question. The card is then flipped over to check the answer and to receive instructions as to how and to where to proceed. Subsequent players follow the same procedure.

Answers can be correct (nondiscriminatory, affirmative action, and/or good business), correct (nondiscriminatory but bad business or not affirmative action) or incorrect (discriminatory) in which case the player must go to Charge of Discrimination, roll the die to determine monetary damages, and return to Jan. 1—all on the same turn.

Each training package is designed to accommodate up to 24 players in a single training session of approximately two to three hours. Ideally, the group should be broken into teams of four to play the game.

One leader who has used the game many times tells us that he has never found a case in which a player makes it all the way to December 31 without getting into some kind of trouble.

CASE STUDIES AND OTHER TYPES OF EXERCISES

When it is easy for the participants to relate case studies and other forms of exercises to the situations in which they operate in real life, an absorbing and effective learning experience takes place. Yet nothing can be more boring or less helpful than when the learner can't easily apply this new experience to his or her own daily problems and job needs.

In his book, *Dynamic Management Education*, Allen A. Zoll, 3rd, provides a wealth of material on in-basket exercises, case histories, and business games of many kinds. The book also contains a useful list of references to sources of additional materials. His discussion of role playing is of special value to group meeting leaders.

Didactic Systems, Inc. Box 457, Cranford, N.J. 07016 also offers a catalog on games and simulations.

THE KEY TO LEARNER INTEREST

I'd like to close this section with a comment Allen Zoll makes in *Dynamic Management Education:* *

> I find the key to learner interest is his active—not passive—participation in the learning process. As the learners state their attitudes or their actions—and their reasons for these (as best they can)—then and only then can they be helped to see their present habits and attitudes and do something about them if they wish to.

---

*Dynamic Management Education (2nd ed.), 1965. Reading, Mass.: Addison-Wesley, p. vii.

QUESTION **22**
HOW CAN YOU MAKE THE BEST USE OF INSTRUMENTS IN GROUP LEADERSHIP?

We hear more and more these days of "instrumentation" in group leadership. This is a new use of an old word in a new situation.

WHAT IS INSTRUMENTATION?

The first picture that may flash across your mind is the complex instruments that face the pilot of a 747 transport—so many instruments that they seem to the passenger to be an unintelligible maze of confusion. Fortunately they don't work that way, at least most of the time.

The American Heritage Dictionary (1973) defines an instrument as "(1) A means by which something is done; agency. (2) One used to accomplish some purpose. (3) A mechanical implement. (4) A device for recording or measuring; especially, such a device as part of a control system. (5) A device for providing music. (6) A legal document"; *AHD* gives as a definition for *Instrumentation:* "(1) The application or use of instruments in the performance of some work."

Somewhere in these dictionary definitions are the roots of the uses of "instrument" and "instrumentation" in the process of group leadership. Certainly instruments are "a means by which something is done, to accomplish some purpose." That purpose may be to create interest and involvement with the members of the group—hopefully to lead to some desired action.

The dictionary tells us, too, that an instrument is "A device for recording or measuring." This is true, too, in the conference or workshop context where instruments are used to provide feedback to the leader and the group members. So let's concoct a definition of an instrument based on these historic roots:

> An instrument used in group meetings is generally a paper-and-pencil device that stimulates interest, involvement, and learning on the part of the participants, and provides feedback to the group and to the leader.

Fortunately, the term "instrument" is flexible and subject to variation depending on the intent of the user. As David Berlo wrote, "meanings are not found in words at all . . . they are found in people."*

A Simple Instrument

Probably the simplest instrument I have used is a pretest–posttest asking the question, "Who Am I?" I use it in a talk on "How the English Bible Came to Us" to adult church groups. (See Table 22.1.)

The test is used as an interest-rouser rather than as a measurement of the present knowledge level of the group. Interest is instant, and attention continues as the group finds the answers to the questions. At the close of the talk, the questions are reviewed and the answers are given correctly by members of the group.

---

*David K. Berlo, 1960. *The Process of Communication.* New York: Holt, Rinehart and Winston, p. 174.

Table 22.1 WHO AM I?

1. I was the subject of St. Paul's shortest letter and probably made the first collection of his letters. Who am I? _____

2. I was a ship owner in Asia Minor who put together the very first New Testament. Who am I? _____

3. We were a group of early Christians who chose death rather than to worship the Roman emperor. We had copies of St. Paul's letters in our church chest. Who are we? _____

4. I am known as the greatest Bible scholar of the early Christian centuries. I put together in six parallel columns the best known Greek and Hebrew translations of the Old Testament. This work is called the Hexapla. Who am I? _____

5. At the request of Pope Damasus, I translated both the Old and New Testaments into Latin A.D. 404. My translation is called the Vulgate and is still used in the Catholic church. Who am I? _____

6. I translated all four gospels into Anglo-Saxon completing the last gospel dictating from my death bed on Ascension Day A.D. 735. Who am I? _____

7. Working with a group of my students, I was responsible for the first English version of the Old and New Testaments. As this was before the discovery of printing, it had to be handwritten on scrolls. Who am I? _____

8. I translated and published the first printed English Bible in 1525 and was strangled and burned for my efforts. I died with the words, "Lord, open the King of England's eyes," on my lips. Who am I? _____

9. I revised and published the first complete English Bible with the royal approval of Henry VIII in 1537 and later helped produce the Geneva Bible in 1560. Who am I? _____

10. I proposed to King James I at the Council of Hampton Court the idea of making a new translation later to be known as the King James Version. Who am I? _____

And a Much More Complex Instrument

Many group leaders over the years have experienced the interest and excitement caused by the Desert Survival and

Subarctic Survival instruments developed by J. Clayton Lafferty, Ph.D., and associates.*

In the Desert Survival situation, group members are asked to rank 15 items according to their importance to survival after a crash landing in the Sonora Desert. First the selection is made individually and then by teams. The results are then checked against the solution by "experts." The exercise shows that when team members work well together, their decision is closer to that of the experts than the decision one member would have made working alone. Minimum time is two hours and interest and involvement are extremely high.

The Subarctic Survival situation is similar to Desert Survival except that group members are told they have crash-landed in the Canadian Subarctic. This experience provides more situational information such as mean temperatures, wind-chill factors, and a map of the area in which the crash occurred. Again, interest is uniformly high. As with Desert Survival, the conclusion is reached that the team can develop more accurate decisions than those made by an individual member working alone. The minimum time for this exercise is also two hours.

Life-Styles Instruments

A series of life-styles instruments developed by Human Synergistics demonstrates the impact of self-concept on individual and group behavior. It utilizes ideas and research from many fields of the behavioral sciences and education to help individuals understand themselves and others better.

The instruments include a Self-Description Inventory and an Interpretation Workbook for use by all levels of management. The inventory is used at two levels: first as a self-analysis and second for analysis by a selected group of seven people who provide candid feedback. A composite profile is prepared by Human Synergistics from these two inputs.

In-depth questionnaires are also provided by Human Synergistics to identify individual motivation and specific

---

*Human Synergistics, 39819 Plymouth Road, Plymouth, Mich. 48170.

work behaviors. Similarities and differences between self-description and feedback from others help management people to understand themselves more fully and to evaluate how well they are doing on the job. This program has helped managers improve their work relationships by clarifying their expectations and increasing awareness of their skills.

Effective use of these instruments requires professional competence and solid understanding of the principles and procedures involved. Composite profiles and recommendations based on them are prepared by the Human Synergistics staff.

Do-It-Yourself Instrumentation

In their book, *Instrumentation in Human Relations Training*, [*] Pfeiffer and Heslin write:

> In our estimation too many people order instruments and then try to adapt them for the group rather than to select the correct instrument for the particular group.

With the wide range of materials and resources available, there is certainly choice enough to fit almost any need. However, it's fun and often effective to develop instruments of your own.

George W. Martin, [†] Management Development Specialist for Blue Cross/Blue Shield of Michigan, has designed a series of simple instruments that he has found useful in creating interest, developing involvement, and furthering the learning process.

Martin writes:

> I think of an instrument as a measuring device. Each item in an instrument helps a participant clarify how he or she thinks about a point, and it provides encouragement to share these thoughts through discussion with

---

[*] J. William Pfeiffer and Richard Heslin, 1973. *Instrumentation in Human Relations Training*. La Jolla, Calif.: University Associates, p.3.

[†] George W. Martin, Blue Cross/Blue Shield of Michigan, Human Resources Planning and Development Division, Detroit. Author of *Let's Communicate*. Reading, Mass.: Addison-Wesley. 1970.

other group members and with the leader. Involvement
leads to increased participation and learning.

If the information is to be shared, care should be
taken that the instrument is nonthreatening to general
discussion. The material should be kept simple and
should not contain irrelevant data.

"Fact or Fallacy."   One instrument that Martin calls "Fact
or Fallacy" is shown in Table 22.2. In this exercise, each individual in the group is asked to circle the number before each
statement that he or she feels is correct. Then the group is
divided into teams of three or four and asked to reach a consensus. When consensus is reached, each team discusses its
findings with the entire group.

Considerably more discussion develops when the individuals make their decisions first, followed by group discussion
and consensus.

"Responsibilities of a Supervisor."   Another Martin "Do-It-
Yourself" instrument is developed around a list of supervisory
responsibilities to be ranked in order of importance by each
individual. Consensus is then reached by discussion in small
groups. Following the group discussion, each member role
plays one of the ego states described on the Transactional
Analysis Workshop Chart in Table 22.3. The main purpose of
this exercise is not to rank the supervisory responsibilities,
but to help the participants become familiar with the TA ego
states.

"Supervisory Skills Instrument."   As a part of the Blue Cross/
Blue Shield Management Development Program, Martin uses
a "Self Diagnosis of Your Supervisory Skills." This is first
completed individually with each person checking those
skills he or she considers important, then rating the ability
with which he or she handles each factor. (See following
pages.) These ratings are then discussed in small groups and
those skills most frequently mentioned are concentrated on
during the remainder of the program.

Table 22.2 FACT OR FALLACY

1. You shouldn't use "I" in business reports.

2. There is a special, formal business language you should use in writing business reports.

3. The average sentence length in a business report should be about 25 words.

4. You should not use contractions in business reports.

5. A good way to make long sentences shorter is to replace connective words such as *and, but, or, because,* and *however* with periods.

6. Outlining before writing is a major key to good report writing.

7. A paragraph shouldn't be shorter than 50 words or longer than 150 words.

8. When you write a report, the main thing you should think about is the audience—the individual or group who will read the report and use the material it contains.

9. There are two main types of reports—informal and formal. The main differences are length, complexity of material, and format.

10. Most formal reports contain these six basic parts (or modifications of them): introduction, summary, body, conclusions, recommendations, and appendix.

11. When writing a first draft, you should complete each section of the report before going on; i.e., you should polish the introduction into final form before beginning to write the discussion.

12. Proofreading your final typed copy for correctness of grammar and spelling is essential. In addition you should ask yourself how it looks, if the pages are in the right order, if it makes sense, if it says what you mean it to say.

Guidelines for Do-It-Yourself Instruments

Here are guidelines for group leaders who wish to develop their own instruments:

Think about your audience.

Think what you want the instrument to accomplish:

- Stimulate discussion
- Generate data
- Facilitate self-disclosure

Table 22.3 TRANSACTIONAL ANALYSIS WORKSHOP

EGO STATES Characteristics	PARENT Critical	PARENT Nurturing	ADULT	CHILD Natural	CHILD Adapted
Tone of voice	Threatening Condescending Accusing Sneering	Patronizing Supportive Sympathetic	Matter-of-fact Confident Clear without undue emotion	Emotional Taunting Whining Loud (fast) Excited	Emotionless Submissive Low
Verbal	You must, have to, should, never, always. You're bad, stupid, slow.	Don't worry. I'm sorry. Are you all right? I understand. Don't feel bad.	Asking for Info: How, what, when, where, who, why? In my opinion. . . . Did you check it out?	Gosh! Wow! Fantastic! Can't—won't I want (need). It's your fault.	Silence Yes sir/ma'am! Whatever you say. Anything else? Excuse making
Manner	Opinionated Always right Lots of talking/ little listening	Tolerant Supportive Encouraging Sympathetic	Paying attention Calm Businesslike Helpful	Imaginative Careless Emotional Spontaneous Curious Self-centered	Withdrawn Inhibited Complying Procrastinating Sulking Rebellious

Facial expression	Scowl Disapproving Frown Pursed lips	Concerned Sympathetic Smiling	Confident Reflective Observing Watching attentively	Teary-eyed Excited Quivering lip Batting eyes	Bored Anxious Worried Expressionless Downcast eyes
Body language	Foot tapping Arms folded Wagging finger Pounding on table Tilted head	Arm on shoulders Pat on back Shaking head to imply OK	Poised Eye contact Natural gestures Nodding head in agreement Head vertical	Slumped Jumps up and down Rigid body Temper tantrum Thumbing nose	Withdrawing Wringing hands Biting nails Avoiding eye contact Shaking head in agreement

If the instrument is to generate data or facilitate self-disclosure, you may be better off to purchase a validated instrument.

Work up a draft (compare with other instruments for ideas on arrangement, scales, etc.).

Try the instrument out on others informally.

Revise where necessary.

Pilot test on small groups. Discuss it with them.

Again revise as necessary.

Develop the final version.

Revise from time to time.

SOME CONCLUSIONS

Experience with these and many other instruments seems to support the conclusion that participants learn more when they are actively involved in the learning process. Instruments provide the group members with a method of specifically focusing on their own behavior.

It is also generally true that when individual thought is followed by group or team discussion, conclusions are more accurate and interest rises to higher levels.

When effectively used, instrumentation can and does create interest and stimulate involvement—and may lead toward desired action on the job. Also, when properly used and followed up, instrumentation provides valuable feedback to the group leader as well as to every member of the group.

RESOURCES FOR INSTRUMENTS

Creative Universal, Inc.
Products Division
21700 Northwestern Highway
Southfield, Mich. 48075

Didactic Systems, Inc.
Box 457
Cranford, N.J. 07016

Human Synergistics, Inc.
39189 Plymouth Road
Plymouth, Mich. 48170

Organizational Tests, Inc.
PO Box 324
Frederickton, N.B.
Canada

Scientific Methods, Inc.
Box 195
Austin, Texas 78767

Teleometrics, Int'l.
2203 Timberloch Place, Suite 104
The Woodlands, Texas 77380

University Associates Publishers, Inc.
7596 Eads Avenue
La Jolla, Calif. 92037

QUESTION **23**

HOW CAN YOU USE GROUP–GENERATED VIDEOTAPE TO ENSURE INTEREST, INVOLVEMENT, AND ACTION?

There is a fascination about "being on the air" that can be used effectively to create instant interest and to ensure involvement in a group situation. There is also a tendency to be "camera shy" when it is a new experience. To convert these tendencies into action back on the job is a challenge to the conference leader.

Dale Madden has met this challenge effectively in his seminar on "Oral Communication Skills" for supervisory and management personnel.[*] Since videotape became available for conference and workshop purposes, Dale has used it to achieve involvement and measurable learning.

HOW THE MADDEN SEMINAR WORKS

Generally, 12 to 20 participants gather at a convenient conference center away from the worksite for a three-day session.

---

[*]Dale J. Madden and Associates, 400 S. Denwood, Dearborn, Mich. 48124.

The climate of the seminar is relaxed with Dale, a very relaxed person, as leader.

During the opening warm-up, the participants are given the opportunity to "interview" the seminar leader. They do this by playing "20 Questions." Each person asks the leader one question (more if a smaller group) like "Who are you?" "Where were you born?" "How did you get to be an 'expert' on communication?" "What are your hobbies?" "Where did you get your education?" etc. By the time they have completed the game, they know the leader quite well—and this point is emphasized. Naturally, this exercise leads to introductions of all the members of the group.

THE APEX FORMULA

Following a minilecture on the nature and importance of effective communication, the leader sets up a basic formula for making an effective oral presentation around the letters A-P-E-X:

A—*Approach*—Gain favorable attention and state need for action.

P—*Proposal*—State proposal to meet the need.

E—*Evidence*—Support or prove idea.

X—*Acceptance*—Call for action, the "X" factor.

Within this framework and supported by examples, the leader introduces an extemporaneous speaking exercise with assigned topics. Ten minutes are allowed for preparation and one minute for presentation.

The First Videotaping

The group is introduced to videotaping by having each member make the extemporaneous one-minute talk before the camera. When all presentations have been taped, they are played back continuously. This gives each participant the opportunity to see and hear himself or herself on the video screen.

The reaction is one of disbelief. "This just can't possibly be me." But the initial fear of being "on camera" like the first plunge into the water is greatly relieved. No individual critique is given on this first time taping. Instead, the members are invited to comment on how well the presenters followed the A-P-E-X formula. Comments are kept brief—and then the group responds to the question:

> "What did you learn about communication from this experience?"

Tips on Talking

Using comments from the group as a base, the seminar leader suggests a number of guidelines for planning and delivering oral presentations:

Talk *to* them—Maintain eye contact.

Easy does it—Make use of natural nervousness to give your presentation "zing!"

They've got you *covered*—Be yourself, not a phony.

Your *slip* is showing—Avoid ums and ahs, throat clearing, etc.

I hear *me*—Keep tuned in on yourself as you talk.

I hear *you*—Keep sensitive to your audience reaction or lack of it.

Team Taping

Closing the first day, the group is divided into teams of four. Each team is given a subject for a five-minute talk to be taped in team fashion like this:

A—*Approach*—Suggest a need (presented by one team member in one or one and a half minutes).   TOTAL

P—*Proposal*—Present the solution (second team member).   5 or 6 minutes

E—*Evidence*—Give backup or proof (third member).

X—*Acceptance*—Call for action (fourth member).

Each team presentation is played back and then discussed for five or six minutes from the standpoints of impact, strengths and shortcomings of the message, probable effect on the simulated audience assumed to be listening. And all this is followed by discussion of the key question:

"What did you learn from this experience?"

By now, the end of the first day, group members have grown in confidence and have overcome the nervousness they felt when they first went "on camera." The big question now is, "How well can I do on the next tape?"

Overnight Assignment

The participants are given a worksheet to guide them in preparing individual five-minute talks for presentation, taping, and critique the next day. Often the people work in pairs in preparing, rehearsing, and refining their presentations. The leader makes clear that the presentations are to be persuasive rather than merely informative and that they are to follow the A–P–E–X formula.

The Second Day

The second day opens with group discussion and a minilecture on the question, "What makes a top-flight presentation?" The discussion centers around ideas like:

- Preparation
- Timing
- Practice
- Delivery
- Enthusiasm
- Use of visuals

For a warmup before taping the presentations, the group presents "The Story of the Bones," an exercise built around a sketch of a skeleton. The "bones" presentation demonstrates the right and wrong ways of using visuals. It is a simple exercise but it gets the point across that visuals are most effective only when properly used.

With the warmup over, one half of the group makes its presentations one after another and each half is taped as they go. The time limit of five minutes is enforced with a one-minute leeway. When the first group has completed its presentations, the presentations are played back and critiqued individually:

- By the presenter answering, "What were my boo-boos?" "What could I have done better?"

- By the group, "How well was the A-P-E-X formula followed?" "What were the strong points and shortcomings?"

- By a summary critique by the leader.

The second half of the group then makes its presentations, and is critiqued in the same way.

Finally, when all have completed their presentations, playbacks, and critiques, the group is asked the question:

"What have you learned from this experience?"

The Final Taping

As a warmup to the final tapings on the third day, the group is given a "fun" exercise. They are divided into teams of four and given the assignment of developing a series of TV shows on wayout subjects such as "Star Wars," "Operation Mars," "Operation Deep Sea," etc. Imagination is the key word. The emphasis is on innovation, use of visuals, and overall interest.

With the group in a fully relaxed mood, the final tapings benefit from the accumulated experience of days one and two. The assignment is a two-minute prepared presentation on a controversial topic of the participant's own choosing. The purpose is to convince and persuade the audience to the presenter's viewpoint. The presentation is followed immediately by a brief question-and-answer period during which the presenter must be prepared to defend the position he or she has taken.

Both the presentation and the question-and-answer session are videotaped and included in the playback. The presenter group, and the instructor view the playback and participate in a constructive evaluation and critique using criteria developed during all three days of the workshop.

A Relaxed and Involved Group

By the final day, the group is interested and involved and are discussing ways they plan to use the A–P–E–X formula when they get back on the job.

Seminar objectives are summarized by the leader:

- To provide you with a method for planning, organizing, and delivering a persuasive presentation using the A–P–E–X formula.

- To deepen your insights into what happens when people communicate.

- To provide skills to improve communication between people.

- To develop additional awareness of the importance of being a good listener.

- To develop self-confidence in your ability to communicate with others.

So, in Summary

The Madden summary provides useful guidelines for making use of group-generated videotapes to ensure involvement and assuring action toward a preconceived objective. In the case of this seminar, the objective is to improve oral communication. The results are real and measurable.

The seminar takes full advantage of the fascination of seeing ourselves on the video screen—and at the same time overcomes stage fright and camera fear by:

- Introducing videotaping very simply with a one-minute extemporaneous talk by each member with a brief and easy critique.

- Providing team experience so that the spotlight can be shared by four team members.

- Providing the A–P–E–X formula so that each participant can follow a logical structure for the presentation.
- Giving plenty of time for planning and rehearsal before the principal presentation.
- Using a three-step method of critique beginning with self-criticism.
- Providing plenty of opportunity to discuss the question, "What did you learn from this experience?"
- Maintaining interest and excitement so that members look forward to using the same methodology back on the job.

Time for Mental Digestion

At first glance, it may seem that too much time is taken in Madden's step-by-step method but this, we feel, is one of the prime reasons that this program has been increasingly successful over the years.

In his little book *Time Out for Mental Digestion*, Robert Rawls* writes:

> To work more effectively with our associates, to get our ideas accepted, to have greater influence with people, we must allow them time out for mental digestion, and we must learn to curb our impatience when they refuse to be swept off their feet by our enthusiasm.

The principle of "the strategic wait" applies with the use of videotape just as it does in any form of conference leadership.

Being in a hurry to have our ideas accepted and adopted is one of our great weaknesses in dealing with people—especially when our objective is to help them acquire a new skill, and to feel good about applying it back on the job. As Aristotle said, "You can learn to do something only by doing it."

---

*Robert Rawls, 1948. *Time Out for Mental Digestion*. Littleton, N.H.: Executive Development Press.

QUESTION 24

HOW CAN YOU EFFECTIVELY TAP INDIVIDUAL TALENTS, EXPERIENCE, AND VIEWPOINTS IN A CONFERENCE GROUP?

In response to this question, Julian W. Moody* told me in a recent taped interview:

> In my experience, the right question asked in the right way, at the right time, and in the right sequence can work wonders in tapping group ideas and experience. Questions trigger the individual's thinking, stimulate creativity, and get the group involved.
>
> Questioning is a fantastic means of learning for all ages, all sexes, and all fields of interest.

There is no magic in any one question or specific series of questions, but questions do seem to have a magic of their own when they are asked in down-to-earth language—not

---

*Julian W. Moody, counselor to management and master of the art of questioning, lives in Santa Barbara, and can be reached through the publisher of this book.

147

textbook talk—and when they relate to the group members *where they are*.

Questions such as "What's most frustrating to you about your job?" will stimulate more thought and participation than "What factors in your job situation do you find most troublesome?" "What's bugging you about your job?" is the kind of question that gets action from supervisory and management people. "What are you trying to get your people to do that's not happening?" creates more involvement than "What's your biggest problem in the supervision of your people?"

FOUR TOOLS THAT CREATE INVOLVEMENT

Four prime tools, when used in the proper combination, create group involvement and lead to learning:

> *Tool 1—Questions*, carefully chosen and expressed, starting from where the group members are, not where you wish they were.
>
> *Tool 2—Chart pages* to record group responses in *Kiplinger Newsletter* style and strung around the room where their impact can be felt.
>
> *Tool 3—A tablet*, preferably yellow and ruled, in front of each participant so that each can *think* and accumulate his or her thoughts for later interchange.
>
> *Tool 4—The group leader's ability* to be sensitive and recognize thought patterns as they emerge, and to distill them into an "essence" to form the basis for consensus and commitment.

CAPSULE OF A CONFERENCE
USING THE MAGIC OF QUESTIONING

Let me create for you the philosophy and the process of a "learning" conference where the magic of questioning opens the minds of the conferees so that they can learn from their own experiences and the experiences of others.

The group is made up of corporate presidents of entre-preneur-type firms. The meeting is held for a single day and is one of a series held over a period of months. All previous sessions had been presented primarily by an expert, followed by the customary Q and A session. They had never before met the leader of today's conference.

They were meeting not to solve an urgent problem or to learn new procedures. They were meeting to learn how they could become more effective in leading their people and their company. They wanted to learn the answer to the question, "What can I do to be a better president in a company that has grown dramatically in the past few years?"

The Starting Point

In opening the meeting, the leader wants to start *where the people are*—not where he or she wishes they were. The leader begins by tuning in on the knowledge of the group members— *what they know*—in order to tie in with this knowledge.

After opening formalities, introductions, etc., the first questions are "Why are you here?" "What do you expect to gain from this meeting?" and "What results do you want to come from this meeting?"

Mental Digestion

The next step in the meeting, and it is critical, is to give the group time to digest their thoughts on these three opening questions. As one conference leader puts it, "I start by giving the group these questions. Then I suggest that they sit at their places around the large square table with their yellow pads in front of them and *just think*. I ask them not to talk with anyone, just sit there and think for five minutes."

This is a hard assignment—and a startling departure from the average "expert presentation" type of meeting. It is the digestion period during which thoughts turn into ideas and contribute to the forward motion of the conference. Without this "thought" period, the questions would lose their power—

and might not lead to the next important step which is involvement.

The Process of Involvement

Questions start people thinking. Then, if the leader lets the
conferees concentrate, ideas will start emerging from the experience, the feelings, the "gut knowledge" of the group.
With this start, the group members are given the opportunity
to share with each other the expectations they had generated
from their own experience. The result is lots of participation
because the group members had to sit there for five minutes
and just *think* about the three simple questions they had
been asked.

The meeting leader records in telegraphic style on the
chart pad the essence of the ideas of each of the group members. This is a crucial step toward attaining the objective
"To effectively tap individual experiences and viewpoints of
the group." The result of this charting might be called the
gross product of the involvement so far, but it needs refine-
ment.

The Refining Process

With all the responses recorded on the chart pages all around
the room, the group needs more time to think. The leader
asks that they sit back and refine the list down to the three
most important factors, based on "gut feeling," and record
these on their yellow pads.

When this process is completed, or the allotted time has
run out, the leader says something like:

> That's a lot of ideas to deal with here in this meeting
> and I have asked you to generate them in 10 to 15
> minutes. Let me ask this, "If we could wave a magic
> wand, and you could get any result you would want
> from this meeting, but only *one* result, what would
> that one result be?"

This sudden shock leads the group to focus sharply on
the assignment. It's a directional question, one that eliminates

fuzzy thinking and, with the leader's guidance, helps arrive at the one thing the group wants most of all to result from this meeting.

The Rationale

The leader is ready now, and only now, to move ahead into substantive areas. Now the leader knows quite precisely where the conferees are in terms of desired results.

Avoiding the pitfall of posing as the expert and outlining the traditional steps in successful management that are found in all the better textbooks, the leader again reaches into the bag of experience of the participants with questions like these:

- What are some essential things that a president should be doing to make a company successful?
- How can we cut through the thousands of ideas we hear and read about and get down to the essentials?

The leader gives the group members time to think about the questions and jot their thoughts down on the yellow pad. Then the leader asks a follow-up directional question like:

- Out of all the things you can think of that have made your business successful, what are the three that you believe are absolutely essential?

After each individual has thought this question through and recorded answers, the conferees discuss their ideas for a few minutes in groups of three. They try to boil their nine ideas into three essential ones. Often these group discussions are held in separate rooms or at poolside.

Emerging Ideas

When the group reconvenes, all the ideas are recorded on the chart pad and refined down to the three or four most important on the basis of group judgment. The leader searches for the "essence" of the thoughts and the presidential needs that have been disclosed.

At this point, the leader may contribute from his or her own management experience, but always in terms of "blending" this experience with that of the group.

The Final Steps

Two important steps remain to make sure that the conference winds up on target—and they are vitally important:

First: Tie the success factors just developed by the conferees to the results expected as established when the meeting started.

Second: Give the members a few minutes to digest what they have learned, and to jot down *for themselves* the action they propose to take when they get back on the job.

Whether that action is to hold regular meetings with top management staff, or whether a more effective management communication linkage is needed, one good idea on how to be a better president will have been well worth the day's work.

Julian Moody has conducted conferences like the one just sketched at many levels of management over the years. They have proved to be effective ways to tap individual talents, and to provide a stimulating learning experience at the management level.

HOW TO TAP INDIVIDUAL TALENTS

It's a long way from company presidents to a little boy in school, but we can't think of a better way to close this chapter than with Helen E. Buckley's poem, "The Little Boy," a poem that points its own moral.

THE LITTLE BOY*

Helen E. Buckley

Once a little boy went to school.
He was quite a little boy.
And it was quite a big school.
But when the little boy
Found that he could go to his room
By walking right in from the outside,
He was happy.
And the school did not seem
Quite so big any more.

One morning,
When the little boy had been in school awhile,
The teacher said:
"Today we are going to make a picture."
"Good!" thought the little boy.
He liked to make pictures.

*Reprinted by permission of Davis Publications, Inc., Worcester, Mass.

He could make all kinds:
Lions and tigers,
Chickens and cows,
Trains and boats—
And he took out his box of crayons
And began to draw.

But the teacher said: "Wait!
It is not time to begin!"
And she waited until everyone looked ready.

"Now," said the teacher,
"We are going to make flowers."
"Good!" thought the little boy,
He liked to make flowers,
And he began to make beautiful ones
With his pink and orange and blue crayons.

But the teacher said, "Wait!
And I will show you how."

And she drew a flower on the blackboard.
It was red, with a green stem.
"There," said the teacher,
"Now you may begin."

The little boy looked at the teacher's flower.
Then he looked at his own flower.
He liked his flower better than the teacher's.
But he did not say this,
He just turned his paper over
And made a flower like the teacher's.
It was red, with a green stem.

On another day,
When the little boy had opened
The door from the outside all by himself,
The teacher said:
"Today we are going to make something with clay."
"Good!" thought the little boy,
He liked clay.

He could make all kinds of things with clay:
Snakes and snowmen,
Elephants and mice,
Cars and trucks—
And he began to pull and pinch
His ball of clay.

But the teacher said:
"Wait! It is not time to begin!"
And she waited until everyone looked ready.

"Now," said the teacher,
"We are going to make a dish."
"Good!" thought the little boy,
He liked to make dishes,
And he began to make some
That were all shapes and sizes.

But the teacher said, "Wait!
And I will show you how."
And she showed everyone how to make
One deep dish.
"There," said the teacher,
"Now you may begin."
The little boy looked at the teacher's dish.
Then he looked at his own.
He liked his dishes better than the teacher's.
But he did not say this.
He just rolled his clay into a big ball again,
And made a dish like the teacher's.
It was a deep dish.

And pretty soon
The little boy learned to wait,
And to watch,
And to make things just like the teacher.
And pretty soon
He didn't make things of his own anymore.

Then it happened
That the little boy and his family
Moved to another house,

In another city,
And the little boy
Had to go to another school.

This school was even Bigger
Than this other one,
And there was no door from the outside
Into his room.
He had to go up some big steps,
And walk down a long hall
To get to his room.

And the very first day
He was there,
The teacher said:
"Today we are going to make a picture."
"Good!" thought the little boy,
And he waited for the teacher
To tell him what to do.
But the teacher didn't say anything.
She just walked around the room.

When she came to the little boy
She said, "Don't you want to make a picture?"
"Yes," said the little boy,
"What are we going to make?"
"I don't know until you make it," said the teacher.
"How shall I make it?" asked the little boy.
"Why, any way you like," said the teacher.
"And any color?" asked the little boy.
"Any color," said the teacher,
"If everyone made the same picture,
And used the same colors,
How would I know who made what,
And which was which?"
"I don't know," said the little boy.
And he began to make pink and orange and blue flowers.

He liked his new school . . .
Even if it didn't have a door
Right in from the outside!

SELECTED REFERENCES

Annual Handbook for Group Facilitators, John E. Jones, Ph.D. and J. William Pfeiffer, Ph.D. (eds). La Jolla: University Associates Publishers.

Berlo, David K., 1960. *The Process of Communication.* New York: Holt, Rinehart and Winston.

Blake, Robert R., and Jane S. Mouton, 1970. *The Grid for Sales Excellence.* New York: McGraw-Hill.

Broadwell, Martin M., 1977. *The Practice of Supervising.* Reading, Mass.: Addison-Wesley.

_____, 1978. *The Supervisor as an Instructor.* Reading, Mass.: Addison-Wesley.

Cantor, Nathaniel, 1961. *Learning through Discussion.* Buffalo, N.Y.: Human Relations for Industry.

Chase, Stuart, 1954. *The Power of Words.* New York: Harcourt, Brace.

Cortwright, Rupert L., and George L. Hines, 1959. *Creative Discussion*. New York: Macmillan.

Dale, Edgar S., 1957. *Audio-Visual Methods in Teaching*. New York: Dryden.

Ellis, William D., and Frank Siedel, 1955. *How to Win a Conference*. Englewood Cliffs, N.J.: Prentice-Hall.

Haney, William V., 1967. *Communication and Organization Behavior*. Homewood, Ill.: Irwin.

Harrison, Jared F., 1978. *Improving Performance and Productivity*. Reading, Mass.: Addison-Wesley.

Hayakawa, S. I., 1949. *Language in Thought and Action*. New York: Harcourt, Brace.

Johnson, Wendell, 1946. *People in Quandaries*. New York: Harper & Brothers.

Korzybski, Alfred, 1948. *Science and Sanity*. Lakeville, Conn.: International Non-Aristotelian Publishing Company.

Lee, Irving J., and Laura L. Lee, 1957. *Handling Barriers in Communication*. New York: Harper & Brothers.

Nichols, Ralph G., and Leonard A. Stevens, 1957. *Are You Listening?* New York: McGraw-Hill.

Pfeiffer, J. William, and Richard Heslin, 1973. *Instrumentation in Human Relations Training*. La Jolla: University Associates Publishers.

Quick, Thomas L., 1976. *Understanding People at Work*. New York: Executive Enterprises.

Rogers, Carl R., and F. J. Roethlisberger, 1952. Barriers and gateways to communication. *Harvard Business Review*, July/August.

Ross, Raymond S., 1977. *Speech Communication: Fundamentals and Practice* (4th ed.). Englewood Cliffs, N.J.: Prentice-Hall.

Whyte, William H., Jr., 1952. *Is Anybody Listening?* New York: Simon and Schuster.

Zelko, Harold P., 1957. *Successful Conference and Discussion Techniques*. New York: McGraw-Hill.

Zoll, Allen A., 3rd., 1969. *Dynamic Management Education*. Reading, Mass.: Addison-Wesley.